Deeper Currents

...

TO CARL —

with gratitude
For your ministry
And GiFT OF
Words —
Bob + Kay
10-11-16

ENGAGING
THE SACRAMENTS
OF HUNTING
AND FISHING

Deeper
Currents

Donald C. Jackson

UNIVERSITY PRESS OF MISSISSIPPI • JACKSON

www.upress.state.ms.us

The University Press of Mississippi is a member of the Association
of American University Presses.

Copyright © 2016 by University Press of Mississippi
All rights reserved
Manufactured in the United States of America

First printing 2016
∞
Library of Congress Cataloging-in-Publication Data

Names: Jackson, Donald C., 1951–
Title: Deeper currents : the sacraments of hunting and fishing / Donald C. Jackson.
Description: Jackson : University Press of Mississippi, 2016. | Description
based on print version record and CIP data provided by publisher;
resource not viewed.
Identifiers: LCCN 2015039714 (print) | LCCN 2015024064 (ebook) | ISBN
9781496805317 (ebook) | ISBN 9781496805300 (cloth : alk. paper)
Subjects: LCSH: Hunting—Anecdotes. | Fishing—Anecdotes. | Human ecology. |
Nature—Religious aspects.
Classification: LCC SK33 (print) | LCC SK33 .J222 2016 (ebook) | DDC
639/.1—dc23
LC record available at http://lccn.loc.gov/2015039714

British Library Cataloging-in-Publication Data available

Portions of this work have appeared in altered forms in the following publications:
"First Light" (2012), "Catalyst for Grace" (2013), and "Before the Storm" (2014), Mis-
sissippi Wildlife Federation, *Mississippi Wildlife*.
"The Purple Plastic Worm" (2013) and "The Vicarious Holy Grail" (2013, originally
published as "The Myth of Control"), American Institute of Fisheries Research
Biologists, *AIFRB Briefs*.

To Don Flynn, my lifelong hunting, fishing, and rambling buddy, who understands, absolutely, the deeper currents

...

Contents

Deeper Currents

...

Catalyst for Grace

...

THE SUN WAS JUST ABOVE THE TREETOPS ACROSS THE RIVER. As it melted into the branches, another blistering day slipped into the cooler stillness of twilight. I could hear the stirring of my companions as they moved between the water's edge where we'd beached our canoes and a spot higher up on the sandbar where we'd established our camp. If by chance there happened to be a puff of breeze during the night, our hope was that the higher spot might catch it. Cicadas whined with a resonating, pulsing rhythm that seemed only to intensify the stillness. The air seemed thick enough to stir with a stick.

A thin, blue-gray wisp of smoke curled slightly and then drifted almost straight up from the young fire one of my companions was tending. He moved like an artist as he studied the blaze. From an imagination only he could grasp, he created something of beauty that reflected his love for the craft. Pausing for long moments, he seemed to peer deeply into the fire, as if there were messages beyond the blaze, much as a sculptor studies stone, stepping back and circling and then carefully adding driftwood branches to strategic spots as the fire's character strengthened, encouraging its evolution toward an ultimate destiny of coals for cooking our supper.

My other two companions were setting up tents so we'd have refuge from mosquitoes while we slept. We were not concerned about rain . . . other than to pray for it during these, the dog days of summer. The waterproofing on the tents was sticky in the heat. Sand patches decorated fabric in spots where the tents had touched earth. From experience I knew that sand would be on everything and in everything—sleeping bags, shoes, cooking pots, utensils, plates, and coffee mugs. There was no avoiding it. It defined our world that evening.

My task was to engage in reconnaissance, to search out a couple of likely spots nearby for trotlines. We didn't want the lines to be too far from camp because we'd be setting them in the dark and would be tending them from time to time throughout the night. It would be too hot, really, to sleep until just before dawn. We would be among the other night creatures out and about, stirring and scrounging and drifting in and out of various encounters with self and beyond.

The sand squeaked under my bare feet as I prowled. I stayed on the edge, walking along the transition zone where water and sand meet. The dry sand was still hot from a day under midsummer sun—much too hot for walking in bare feet. But I liked the way it felt underfoot, so walked in it as long as I could before stepping over into the shallow water to keep from cooking my toes and heels.

I've always loved sandbars. When fresh and untrammeled they speak to me of the physical forces that created them. They are incredibly dynamic. All are unique. Their forms are full of swirls and fragile edges, tapering into transition zones, then fading away. They are in synchrony with the rhythms of seasons and obedient to sculpturing by wind and water. Their ephemeral beauty captivates me, forever drawing me back into their realm, forever strengthening my love affair with lowland southern rivers.

The dank and pungent odor of a dead gar mellowing in the sand just above the waterline added its essence to the thickness of the evening air and caught my attention. I didn't mind the smell. Call me weird, but the richness of decay, flora or fauna, is not offensive to me. Perhaps, with the years, I've come to accept and understand a little better its purposes as life ebbs and flows, regenerates and resurrects. Frankly, and in my opinion, a sandbar isn't really a sandbar unless there is at least one dead gar on it. I stopped to check this fellow out, to see what species it might be. Its long beak was the distinguishing character, a dead (no pun intended) giveaway: long-nose gar, one of the more common gars in this region. And this was a good one, almost four feet long. When alive, it probably weighed ten to fifteen pounds, perhaps more.

As I looked at that old dead gar I couldn't help but think a little about how much I like gars. I like to fish for them. They're good fighters if you can actually hook them. I like to eat them too. Their back straps make good fish sticks for frying or grilling, and when cut into chunks they are perfect for stir-fry dishes, with the texture of shrimp and a wonderful flavor all their own. In our southern streams they serve a critical role as mid-water predators, helping to structure fish populations. They were on earth before humans came on the scene and will likely still be here after we're gone. Something about that gives me a good feeling. . .

I moved out of my moments of reflections about gars and energy flows and the theology of a naturalist and focused again on the task at hand. Across the river there was a steep dirt bank laced with vines and toppled-down trees. Some of the trees were in the water. From where I stood I could faintly make out some larger (hopefully solid and strong) branches on those old snags, places where we could tie our trotlines. There also were a couple of good spots among the snags for stretching the lines. We had two trotlines, so that's all we needed—just two good spots. I could almost sense catfish in that dark water starting to stir.

It was going to be a perfect night. Hot, muggy, still. Yep, an absolutely perfect night for a sandbar camp and some trotlines. I slapped at a mosquito, then turned and went back to camp, and as I did so I started thinking back across the years about trotlining . . . its place within the culture of the Deep South and what it has always meant to me.

Trotlining for catfish in the Deep South is so deeply engrained as a cultural icon that we hardly even talk about it. It is just done. It falls into the same category as setting up a coffeepot at a hunting camp or saying grace at the table. It typically isn't the main focus of the event, but leave it out and something just isn't right . . . and you're likely to hear about it. Most of us have a trotline or two stashed away with our outdoor gear, behind the seat of our pickup trucks, in our "survival pack," or wadded up in a plastic freezer bag down in a tackle box. I have two that have been in my life for over fifty years.

When I was a kid, the lake I lived by had strict rules about fishing. One of those rules was "no trotlines." All fishing was to be done with rod and reel. The lake was full of channel catfish but nobody really fished for them. Everybody seemed to fish for bass, bream, and, occasionally, crappie. I didn't see any sense in the rule and so deliberately embarked on a life of crime. At the age of twelve I became a poacher.

I constructed two trotlines that gathered on big twelve-inch-long safety pins that I made out of wire clothes hangers. I tied twenty twelve-inch loops along the main line at thirty-inch intervals to comply with state regulations. I obeyed state rules, just not the local, misguided, lake rules. These loops served as my drop lines that would hold the hooks. The thirty-inch distance between the drop lines keeps most hooked fish from getting tangled up with each other. At the end of each drop line I threaded a grommet through which I'd drop hooks when I was ready to set the line. Otherwise, the hooks stayed in a pouch on my belt and the grommets were strung along the safety pin. All I had to do is open the pin and the grommets would slide off in good order. I never had a tangle. I didn't need swivels because the eyes of the hooks rotated on the grommet openings.

With a little practice I could stretch the line in just a few minutes, tie it off, and come back along it, hanging my hooks through the grommets and simultaneously baiting the hooks. I could put out a twenty-hook line in less than ten minutes and take it up in less than fifteen minutes, unless, of course, there were fish on the line. Speed in deployment and retrieval were important to me as a budding poacher. I'd set my lines just before I'd go to bed at night and run them the following morning, just after I finished my paper route and before I had to go to school.

The reality was that nobody really cared that I was running trotlines in the lake. In fact, they sort of encouraged me. Had I known this at the time, the sweetness of living a criminal life would have faded. It wasn't until years later that I learned that most folks in the community knew about what I was doing and were sort of amused by it. Some figured that the more experience I got on the water the more likely I was to accept the truth regarding my identity—and someday become a fisheries biologist, which I did. As the twig is bent, so grows the tree. I think that one of the reasons I ultimately became a fisheries biologist was so that I could catch fish with what would otherwise be illegal gear—all sorts of lines, traps, nets, electricity, and sometimes even explosives! I was our community's young "Robin Hood," catching "the king's" fish and giving them away to folks who needed or wanted them.

Boy, did I ever catch a lot catfish on those trotlines! Sometimes the rickety old boat I used would be squirming full of nice channel catfish. Once in a while I'd even catch a flathead catfish. The channels would weigh up to around two or three pounds on average. The flatheads would usually run up to around eight to ten pounds. Sort of small for the species, but they were huge to me.

Back then my father was a Protestant minister at a local church. My mother was an elementary school teacher at the neighborhood school. Preachers and teachers in the Deep South didn't earn much in the 1960s and there were four of us kids in the parsonage. Both of my parents were products of the Great Depression of the 1930s and, like most people in our community, they either didn't know or didn't care what the fishing rules were on the lake. Both had experienced hunger before, and, in fact, we as a family had dealt with some of that in my younger years, while my father was in seminary up in Kentucky.

When I got old enough to fish by myself, I got a clear, albeit tangential, understanding that my father adhered to and promoted Jesus's admonition, "Feed my sheep," which in my youthful theology I interpreted as feeding my mother, my two sisters, my little brother, me, and anybody else around who wanted a mess of fish. My father's encouragement, grounded in scripture, set me on fire. But, since I couldn't do miracles to feed the masses, I had to compensate by catching lots of fish.

I remember once coming home late with a wet burlap bag full of fish and being somewhat under the wrath of those who had been home for a while doing "my" chores while I was off fishing. My father stepped in, defending me, saying, "Back off, he's bringing in the bacon isn't he?" Those trotlines often made the difference in my family's wellbeing ... especially toward the end of the month.

My two trotlines stayed close at hand throughout my youth and were regularly used beyond the "home" lake. When I got old enough to venture out beyond our community, rafting on rivers, shooting ducks on old sloughs, breaks, and derelict rice reservoirs, or camping on squirrel hunts or on hikes, my trotlines continued to "bring in the bacon." I discovered early on during these forays that duck guts and squirrel livers were outstanding channel catfish bait. If I could get live bait like small sunfishes, I could catch flathead catfish. I'd cut a cane pole, bait up with worms or crickets I'd scrounge nearby, catch some small sunfish, and then, buddy, watch out! Flathead catfish—Ho!

In the backwater areas and in smaller creeks I'd also catch bullhead catfish on my lines. In some of the larger rivers I'd catch blue catfish. The species of catfish didn't matter to me. I realized that a person with a trotline in the Deep South need never go hungry. When I was out on my wild forays and there was a place and a way to set a trotline, I certainly didn't go hungry. Neither did those who ventured with me.

And so I proceeded with my task as "trotline master" on this wonderfully still, muggy, and mosquito-infested night as my companions set up camp and tended the fire. They had faith in me. I had faith in the river to provide. Although constantly under threat of destruction by misguided souls in the South who don't know rivers, the river we were on this evening (as are many others throughout the region), was still there, in good shape, and full of fish for the taking, fish for the sandbar camps . . . fish for *our* sandbar camp.

The fire was mellowing by the time I returned to camp. The sun was throwing its last rays of soft, mushy gold across the treetops. I dug into my gear, got my lines and hooks, and then went to the ice chest to get a freezer bag that contained nuggets of deer liver—also an outstanding bait! The fire tender couldn't be lured from his art, so one of the tent-stake-pounders volunteered to paddle the canoe as I stretched the line. By the time we slipped the canoe into the river it was dusky dark.

The snags I'd selected for the sets were less than a hundred yards from our camp. We pushed the canoe out into the current and drifted down to the first one. The river was low. The current barely swirled among the branches. It wasn't difficult to keep the canoe in position as I tied one end of the first line to a branch. Then we let the canoe drift slowly downstream. As it did, I played out the line, allowing the grommets to slip off of the wire safety pin. When we got to the end of the line I tied on a length of cotton twine and we stretched it out until we could tie it to another branch. Then we slowly paddled back along the length of the line. While my companion handled the canoe, I slipped a hook into each of the grommets and baited the hook. In less than ten minutes the line was set and baited. Fifteen minutes later the second line was out and baited and we returned to camp.

In some ways, trotlining is a little like trapping. Your mind is full of imaginings about what's going on "out yonder." The critters are stirring, sniffing, testing, getting bolder and bolder, and then they commit and you've got them! You never know just what you've got, however, until you go check. You want to go check very badly and too soon. But, you've got to give the traps or the lines some time. You've got to find something else to do or to think about.

That's actually impossible. Even when you're busy cooking supper or messing around with whatever gear you may have with you, you're always casting a wayward look toward where the action is. Try as you might, you end up stumbling around camp, knocking dishes and cups off logs, not paying attention to where tent-stake lines are pegged to the ground, and ignoring direct questions.

You're lost in the dreamtime and there's no cure. You're out in those bushes or deep in the currents.

With trapping, you've got to leave things alone all night long. It doesn't serve you well to get out there among the critters and stir them up. But with trotlining, checking every hour or so works just fine and wards off nervous frustration.

So, after supper and a little fireside chat, when I couldn't stand it any longer and was about to go mad and bite myself, I got up from the driftwood log I was sitting on, calmly stretched a bit, and said, "Well . . . I reckon I'll go check the lines. Anybody want to help?"

Although it does not take two canoes to check a trotline, two canoes and four grown men went out into the dark of the night, onto that delicious, swirling, muddy old river. Once on the water, flashlights probed the thick air. We could see the beams as diffuse vectors in the dark. Then there was a call from the lead canoe, "Line's twitching! We've got something!"

It is sort of like Christmas morning when you approach a twitching, throbbing trotline. You know there's something in the package, you just don't know what it is—and it doesn't matter! The line is grabbed and worked down to where the hooked fish is. Then, with splashing and twisting, the fish is hauled onboard— wonder of all wonders, and they all are—a beautiful wild fish flopping in the bottom of a canoe, glistening in the beam of a flashlight, working those sharp pectoral spines that stick out on both sides just behind the head, making a sort of grating, almost grunting sound to warn you that it means business and you'd better know what you're doing if you grab on.

This first fish of the night was a fine channel catfish that weighed about four pounds. Out came the pliers, the fish was securely grabbed, and the hook twisted out. Then we placed it on the bottom of the canoe. It squirmed a little until it felt comfortable, then lay still, whiskers twitching, gill opercula flapping.

"Hey, y'all, we've got another 'un down here." And so we had, another fine channel catfish that weighed about two pounds. The second line held one fish, a small blue catfish that weighed perhaps a pound. Its fine, small head, humped back, and steely blue color contrasted sharply with the more sleek and silvery-sided and spotted "chuckleheaded" channel catfish we'd caught. We couldn't have been more pleased. These fish were more than enough for the breakfast we envisioned for the following morning.

We heard a smack then and knew we had beaver nearby. Casting our lights across the water around us, we spotted one of the rascals cruising along the shoreline. Farther down the bank a pair of eyes glowed. It was a raccoon hunting whatever, probably crayfish and the odd frog. The air was noticeably cooler out here on the river and, as a result, by the time we started back to camp there was a light fog over the water. Paddling through the fog was wonderfully surreal. It was as if we were the only people on earth. And in some ways, we were. We'd not seen another soul our entire trip. The river was ours, and ours alone. That in itself has always amazed me.

I've always wondered why there are not more people out doing river stuff, camping, fishing, trotlining, canoeing. But then, as we were paddling back, I thought to myself, "I'm sort of glad that there aren't. It's wilder this way, and it is the wild that lures me to be here again and again and again . . ."

After we beached the canoes, we killed and filleted our fish and put the fillets in the ice chest to cool. Leaving the fish on a stringer overnight was out of the question. That would only invite trouble from prowling critters in the river and on land. Plus, the water was so warm that these fish probably would die if put on a stringer and be wasted. They wouldn't be able to move enough to keep enough of the warm water passing over their gills. Were the water cooler, then they might make it overnight on a stringer. But in midsummer they probably wouldn't. We wanted fish fillets for breakfast.

The owls called to us, reminding us of the hour, and we drifted off to our tents for hot and restless sleep. Once inside the tents, and after the mosquitoes that had come in with us had been systematically discovered by flashlight and killed, we lay on top of our sleeping bags, covered with sweat and sticky. Although there was a screen door and screen window in the tent, there was no air movement. The nylon sleeping bags stuck to our bare skin. Sweat trickled and dripped. But within an hour the night had cooled enough that the sweating had stopped. I could hear snoring in the other tent. Soon thereafter I drifted off into never-never land.

The owls called again just before sunrise. I'd been awake on top of my sleeping bag for a while, waiting for their invitation to get up and get going. When I unzipped the tent and went out to see the new day, I saw the fire artist again at work, resurrecting his masterpiece and preparing to pour fresh coffee from the pot. He'd been up for some time. Nothing was said. But a cup of strong coffee was handed to me. There are certain sorts of companions who are precious in a camp.

"There are fish on the lines," he said after I'd taken a couple of sips of coffee. "I just had to go out and look, but I left them for y'all to see."

I looked across the water and, through the light, misty fog that hung over it, I could see the end of one of the trotlines bobbing and twitching. A crow cawed. The owls answered. A pair of wood ducks whipped along over the river channel and disappeared around a bend. Our other two companions were beginning to stir in their tents.

Another sip of hot coffee . . . then a grin as the first fillet hit the bacon grease in the skillet. I looked around me at the sandbar, the fog-covered river, the twitching line, our canoes, and the camp. I smelled the wood smoke and the coffee and heard my companions as they greeted the new day with laughter and ribbing. It was then that I thought to myself, "Trotlines, truly they are wonderful catalysts for grace."

And the line across the river twitched and jerked again.

Home Is the Mariner

...

WE WERE YOUNG THEN, FLUSH WITH THE VIBRANCY OF OUR masculine sunrise. The world was all before us. We could feel its swell around us, within us, between us as we forged ahead—four high school boys, Mike Kelly, Aniel House, Don Flynn, and me—heading out for a squirrel hunt along Wattensaw Bayou, one of the small tributaries of the White River, near the little community of Hazen in eastern Arkansas.

A plume of dust trailed Don's Dodge Dart on the gravel road. Frost sparkled on roadside grass and bushes. The sun was already touching the uppermost branches of the trees. We were late for a typical squirrel hunt, and we knew it, but we really didn't care and weren't in a rush. We were off adventuring on a fine Saturday morning, and that was all that mattered. Plus, we had a different sort of hunt planned. An early start wouldn't work for what we had in mind.

The road we followed that late October morning was only passable after the river had rested for a while within its main channel. It was a restless river, one that frequently flexed its muscle. When it did, the entire region felt its power. Sometimes it could be a monster. At other times it was a dark and mysterious jewel flowing through an emerald forest, with sandbars flashing in sunlight and snags that whispered deep secrets ... and we loved that river.

We loved it for all that it was and for all that it created. During its ravages it carved the landscape, ripping, tearing, digging, throwing sand and mud and silt over its entire floodplain. When resting in its channel, it called to us with a primeval message that resonated in our very souls. And when we heeded the call, it revealed wilderness treasures that seemed to come from the realm of dreams. Personified, it was for us something akin to our amorphous images of a wizard, perhaps even a god, for through the millennia its forces had been almost magical, creating a maze of anastomosing channels and backwaters with connections that varied in concert with the river's mood.

The land also was restive, responsive not only to the river but also to seasons. During those years the forest was primeval, with towering cypress, oak, gum, and cottonwood. Shadows were deep. Spirits lurked in the deeper ones. Life oozed and swelled and crawled and climbed and darted in myriad forms.

Sirens called to young men like us, young men as restless as the river, as restive as the land. We heard those sirens, listened carefully, and were drawn ever closer to their source. We prowled and probed, afoot, afloat ... slipping through the forests and along the waterways, fishing, hunting, and rambling. We sloshed and waded and mucked our way through this paradise, listening not only to the sirens but also to the songs that swelled within our youthful hearts. We were like the river—ebb and flow, ebb and flow, in and out—time and again penetrating and withdrawing, in rhythm with something beyond earth, wind and sky.

The crunch of gravel faded to a softer whisper of tires on dust. The road was a road no longer but only a lane pockmarked by occasional ruts from wetter times. Then it became a faint track through grass and woods. Finally, where the true forest began, the track ended in a small, gravel-covered area under the trees. We parked the car there. The bayou was down through the woods, about a hundred yards or so away from where we'd parked.

Although it was only sunrise, it felt "late." We could already hear squirrels barking back in the woods. But we didn't care. We had a different strategy for today's hunt. This was not going to be a typical "disperse in the woods in the predawn dark and be back at the vehicle at noon" sort of hunt. No sir, we'd developed a plan that we knew absolutely would take us to the mother lode of squirrels. There was going to be a squirrel massacre that morning. It was foolproof. And, to make it all the sweeter, our new strategy would take us far away from the crowds.

In reality, there was no crowd. We were the only hunters there that morning. In fact, we typically were the only squirrel hunters who ever hunted this area. Rarely did we see anyone else. Rarely was there even a vehicle parked down where we were in the woods by the bayou. But reality, history, and data were lost on us. We already had visions firmly planted in our heads. We had created our own reality. We were leaving the trampled, worn out, shot out, over hunted land, and were headed straight for the frontier where fox squirrels virtually dripped from the branches and vines, and gray squirrels swarmed like blackbirds in oak and wild pecan trees. We were of a single mind, in pursuit of the holy grail of squirrels.

Our strategy centered on a little wooden boat that Aniel had made two summers earlier in his father's woodworking shop. Being not quite sixteen years old at the time, too young to get a paying job, he didn't have much else to do that summer and so decided (or rather his father decided) that he needed a project. There had been construction plans for this little boat published in an issue of *Popular Mechanics*. Aniel's father had both the plans and the necessary tools . . . and presented them in no uncertain terms to Aniel.

So, now there was this boat and, of course, boats are magic things. They fan the dreams of boys. They become pirate ships or French Voyager canoes or landing craft in a war zone, carrying artillery (water balloons) to attack the forces on the beach (girls sunbathing on the edge of a local lake). Occasionally, they are used for more practical purposes, like fishing or hunting. Now, on this Saturday morning, we'd be using that little boat to get us beyond what we considered "worn out" squirrel-hunting territory—anything within a mile of the parking place there at the end of the road. Never mind that the woods around us there at the parking place was at that moment a virtual storm of squirrels barking and thrashing the branches over our heads and that this storm of squirrels continued for as far out into the woods as we could see.

Our plan was to transport two hunters across Wattensaw Bayou to "virgin" territory, and then the other two hunters would float down the bayou in the boat, shooting squirrels from the boat as it drifted silently with the current. We had my little 1963 Johnson 3-horsepower outboard motor to travel back to our launching point after the hunt.

It would be a grand venture and we were primed for it. We'd brought a large cooler full of ice along with us and left it ready and waiting back in the car. We figured we'd need that ice chest to keep all of our squirrels in after the hunt so that they would remain fresh during the drive back to North Little Rock. We'd also brought along extra shotgun shells, two boxes apiece. That's fifty shotgun shells. The daily limit of squirrels then was eight.

After crawling out of Don's car and stretching a bit, we unlashed and unloaded the boat from where we had it stuffed in the trunk of the car. It only stuck out the back of the trunk about four feet. As I said before, it was a *small* boat. When we took it out of the trunk we found that the latch on the bottom of the car's trunk had busted a hole in the bottom of the boat as we'd bounced down the road to the woods. But we were prepared for such mishaps and quickly repaired the hole with two strips of duct tape. Then we each grabbed a corner of the boat and, commando style, carried the boat through the woods and down across the slippery, muddy bank of the bayou to our launching spot.

The boat was made from marine plywood and held together by wood screws. It was, as a result, solidly built and after construction had been properly soaked so that the seams had swelled and were watertight. We figured our duct tape over the new hole would also be watertight, at least for the duration of this day's venture. We had great confidence in the boat's builder, in the little motor, in the seaworthiness of the craft, and in the seamanship of the crew. As long as nobody leaned to the sides or to the front or to the back, or shifted weight while aboard, we'd be just fine.

With the boat in the water and secured to a tree trunk with a length of rope, we went back to the car for our guns and other gear. Don carried my shotgun along with his own so that I could carry the little outboard motor down to the boat.

It was a gorgeous but cold morning. The sky was the deepest of blue. The forest was ablaze with color. As we'd entered this area I'd noticed that the sloughs and ditch channels and bayous were low and that many were dry, or almost so, with only residual pools of dark, leaf-stained water. Fortunately, however, Wattensaw Bayou still had some current and enough deep water to float our boat. In fact, as we were later to learn, it was plenty deep.

I breathed the chilled autumn air and stood still for a few moments before taking the motor down to the boat, reconnecting with the earth and with myself, a "semi-feral" young man of sorts. Memories of my former hunts in this area swirled in my mind and my heart. I'd hunted here many times before and was deeply in love with this forest and its watery ways. It was such an ancient forest, a forest that, as far as I knew, had never been touched in any significant way by saw or ax. When I was in that forest, the timelessness of the place became the deepest current I traveled on. It wasn't the hunting or the fellowship or the adventure that lured me back again and again, as wonderful as they were, but rather those deeper currents. They were the sirens' song.

I did, however, also love the hunting, especially the squirrel hunting, because it linked me with that forest in so many ways. During my hunts I'd ramble for miles and miles, just probing and watching and never really worrying about getting lost, and really not that concerned about shooting many squirrels, although at times the squirrel hunting had been fabulous. I shot plenty but also let many go.

Hunting squirrels in this forest was pretty special because for six months each year the forest completely shaded the ground, with only an occasional dimple of sunlight making it all the way to earth. Then, during winter and early spring, floodwaters covered much of the area. As a result of shade and flood there was practically no undergrowth. The ground was covered by a carpet of leaves and accumulated organic debris. Under that carpet the ground was soft and new and fertile. It was so soft, in fact, that it was easy to sneak up on a squirrel. I could stalk with almost no noise at all.

Although capable of being raucous teenagers, in this cathedral we rarely spoke beyond whispers. Twigs crunched softly underfoot as they were pressed into the soft ground. Pileated woodpeckers occasionally broke the hush with their haunting calls . . . calls that seemed to echo but really didn't. Near the bayou there was a flooded depression with some open water. Now, more than half an hour after sunrise, herons and egrets flashed white, gray, and blue as they flew up from that backwater, their images reflected perfectly on the still surfaces.

As we walked the hundred or so yards from the car to the boat, carrying our gear and guns, we were surrounded by the forest's giant pillars. Some of the trees were so large that it took all four of us to circle their trunks with our arms. Their canopies high overhead occasionally rustled ever so slightly as they were brushed by autumn breezes. In the wetter places there were cypress knees taller than a man's head.

As carefully as I could, I attached the little outboard motor to the transom of the tiny boat. It was my motor, so I was to be the captain. I'd transport Aniel and Mike across the bayou one at a time. Then, after they were on the other side, Don would join me in the boat and we'd do our float hunt.

The front of the boat had a small compartment for storing supplies like shotgun shells, rope, and drinking water. The compartment was covered by plywood, but the plywood board wasn't intended to serve as a seat because the front of the boat angled up at a slant that wouldn't allow enough freeboard if someone was actually at the front of the boat.

Aniel knew about these features of the boat. He'd built the thing. So when he got into the boat he hunkered down right in the center of the bottom and carefully held on to the sides to help with balance. I started working with the motor, trying to get it started. It was a cantankerous old motor, especially when cold, and in spite of my efforts, I couldn't get it to start. While I was trying to start the motor, Aniel brought out one of the boat's paddles and worked the boat over to the opposite shore of the bayou. I felt the boat bump the opposite bank so quit trying to start the motor, stabilized the boat, and helped Aniel get out and up the steep bank.

Then I paddled over to pick up Mike. Mike got into the boat and, unknown to me, immediately went to the front and sat down on that piece of plywood, thinking it was a seat. I had my back to him while I tried again to start the motor. Every time I pulled on the starter cord I'd hear Mike mumbling something but couldn't make out what he was trying to say. He kept saying something about water on the seat. It didn't matter to me. Wet seats are just part of being in a boat.

But it *should* have mattered, because what Mike was trying to tell me was that every time I pulled on the starter cord, and the boat move forward a little, there was water coming over the front of the boat. Finally, I gave the starter cord one good strong pull and the motor roared to life.

Immediately, the boat did a nosedive down into Wattensaw Bayou. The next thing I saw was Mike swimming with one hand, his shotgun held high over his head with his other hand, heading to the opposite bank, where Aniel stood laughing. I'm taller than Mike and was actually standing on the bottom of the bayou with water up to my neck. The boat was filled with water, but upright and still floating. It was drifting toward the shore where we'd launched. Don was in the process of trying to catch it, but was laughing so hard that he was stumbling and at risk of slipping into the bayou to join me.

Mike was furious, but we all took Mike's fury in stride. He was famous for his Irish genes. I was shocked by the cold water but unhurt and safe. Aniel and Don were rolling on the ground, seemingly unable to catch their breath from laughing. I swam and sloshed my way over to where Don was trying to grab the boat. Man the water was cold!

I looked across the bayou and could see Mike transforming from shock and rage to hypothermia. He stood there, thoroughly soaked, draped in a double bandolier of shotgun shells, his old army campaign hat the only dry thing on his body, his gun still dripping water, and him on the wrong side of the creek.

I knew that I needed to go back across the bayou and get Mike, and then get him warmed quickly. I also needed to get warmed up. As quickly as I could, and with Don's help, we captured and bailed the boat. Then I paddled across for Mike. I offered to haul Aniel back too, but he said he'd just stay over there for a while and hunt, if he could stop laughing . . .

When Mike and I got back over to the launch side of the bayou, we secured the boat and went with Don to the car to look for matches. We finally found some and built a fire from driftwood. But in our soaked clothes, we were not getting warmed up. So I stripped and Don, bless his heart, did too. He peeled off his white, insulated underwear, handed it to me, and dressed again. Mike, being a bit more conservative, decided to keep his old wet clothes on rather than strip out in front of God and everybody, or take clothes offerings from his hunting buddies. He just hunkered down closer to the fire.

Once I put on Don's insulated underwear, I warmed quickly. The morning was still young and the sirens still called my name. So, dressed in white, long-handled underwear, I grabbed a handful of shotgun shells, stuffed the shells under my hunting hat (the underwear had no pockets), grabbed my shotgun, and went stalking off into the woods for my squirrel hunt.

The squirrels apparently had never seen a hunter in white, insulated underwear walking through the woods. In fact, they seemed to be completely baffled by what they saw and would expose themselves (just like me), trying to figure out what in the

world it was that was invading their world. I helped them understand. In about forty-five minutes I'd shot three big fox squirrels.
That was enough for me. I returned to the fire, and to Mike . . .

Mike was still cold but not shaking quite as much as before.
He was very quiet, sitting on a log, poking the fire. I heard the
outboard motor running and went down to the bayou to investi-
gate. There was Don, driving that little boat around. He looked
up at me and grinned. He obviously wasn't hunting, or else he'd
have been paddling, not running the motor. I just waved him off,
turned back toward the fire, and rejoined Mike. The sound of
the motor eventually faded and I assumed Don was going off in
search of quieter places for his squirrel hunt. I figured that he'd
be OK. A couple of hours later, after Mike had warmed some and
was actually beginning to dry out a bit, I heard the motor again.
A few minutes later, the sound of the motor quit and then Don
and Aniel came to the fire. Aniel had four squirrels. Don had one.

About this time, Mike, perhaps aided by anticipation of leaving
for home, began to see the humor in our nautical mishap, and even
started chuckling. That's all it took for the rest of us. It doesn't take
much to get seventeen-year-old boys laughing. As we caught our
breath time and again, we went over the entire episode, recounting every detail, laughing until our sides hurt. We then, finally, all
pitched in, doused the fire, loaded up the boat, the motor, and all
the other gear, and headed back home.

The boat never went on another hunt. And, even though we
loved that place and continued to tell the stories until they became
legends, we never went back as a group to Wattensaw Bayou. It
wasn't something planned or something deliberate. We always
thought we'd go back, but it just didn't happen. Our squirrel
hunts there were passages . . . a chapter in our lives; the boat

event marked that chapter's end. In fact, after the boat adventure with Mike, Aniel, and Don, I didn't return to Wattensaw Bayou for more than forty years.

Then one day, when I was sixty years old, traveling back from North Little Rock to my home in Mississippi, I started thinking about Wattensaw Bayou, of the days spent there alone and with friends, and wondering what it might look like now. I had a dog, a shotgun, a pair of boots, and some shotgun shells with me in my pickup truck. I'd been duck hunting with Don for a few days on land we'd leased that season and really wasn't in any sort of hurry at all.

It was one of those gorgeous midwinter afternoons in Arkansas when the sun is just right, the temperature is in the lower 50s, and there is no wind. It was a perfect afternoon for rambling, perfect for reconnections. The closer I got to the Hazen exit off the interstate leading to Memphis, the more I thought about those days long ago when we'd roamed the forests as boys along Wattensaw Bayou. By the time the Hazen exit was visible in the distance, my decision had been made. I switched on the truck's turn signal, slowed down, took the exit off the interstate highway, and engaged my automatic pilot.

I wasn't sure how to get to the road that led to our old hunting haunts. All I could remember was that to get to Wattensaw Bayou I had to turn left off the exit ramp, go back across the interstate bridge, and head north. I couldn't remember how far it was to the turnoff or how far it was from the turnoff down to the bayou.

Then an old internal compass clicked in and soon I *knew* that I was on the right path. As I drove, my pickup truck seemed to have a mind of its own. The pace and the turns seemed so natural. A gravel road came into view and I turned on it as if I were turning into the driveway of my home. I knew it was the right road. In fact, in many ways I *was* turning into the driveway of one of my spiritual homes.

I followed that gravel road as it wound through the countryside and then started going deeper and deeper into forest. I could feel the bayou's pull. I could hear the sirens calling my name in a sea of memory and emotion. It felt so right.

The trees were bigger than I remembered, but with each turn I knew I was getting closer and closer to the old place. I felt a thrill swelling within me, a special sort of chill that comes over me when I'm in the presence of God and doing the right thing. I started remembering, more and more clearly, the turns, the rises, the low spots, and then—suddenly, before me, as I passed through a wrinkle in time—there was the old parking place. It was still there and it was gorgeous.

Memories washed over me, flooding me with emotion. I got out of my car and was within moments on my knees, alone in prayer . . . a prayer of thanksgiving for a youth well spent here in this forest so long ago and for a life that had allowed me the gift of returning. I smelled the deep, dank, smell of the earth, a smell that is unlike earth smell anyplace else in the world. I heard the call of pileated woodpeckers. A fox squirrel jumped from the ground at the edge of the parking area and flattened itself against the trunk of an ancient oak. I felt the stillness, the timelessness.

I got back on my feet, returned to my truck, and let my dog out. Then I put on my boots, grabbed my shotgun and a handful of shotgun shells, and started walking through the forest, through a couple of damp swales, and then down toward the bayou. The closer I got to it the stronger the bayou's pull was on me. I felt energy surge deep within me as I took the last few steps to the bank. I hesitated, took a deep breath, and went right to the edge.

There it was, beautiful, dark, gently flowing, full of mystery. I became very still and listened for its voice. Leaves spun on its surface. Memories spun in its depths. Then I could hear it whispering. It spoke to me just as it had back when I had ventured here as a boy. It welcomed me home. A slight afternoon breeze, the first of the day, moved the topmost branches of the ancient trees, and they too—the wind and the trees—spoke to me, asking why I had been gone for so long . . . and I had no answer to that question.

I turned and walked upstream along the bayou, through the small patches of cane and among the cypress knees. The giant pillars of oaks and cypress that had been there in my youth were now huge beyond imagining.

Then I paused again and listened even more intently. I looked at the forest around me, soaking up the primal essence of the land. I shut my eyes. I felt the rhythms of earth meld with my internal rhythms . . . just as they had done so many years ago during my youth. Something beautiful, something stirring and wonderful came back to life—like whispers unleashed into a symphony—and I understood.

Anchored by the ancient forest and blessed in baptism by an equally ancient river, the earth here along Wattensaw Bayou spawns and nurtures a species of phoenix that rises perpetually, not from ashes, but from floods, silt, and debris, forever becoming . . . forever returning.

And so it was for this phoenix, this old Wattensaw mariner, as he called his dog, slung his shotgun across his shoulder, and turned back toward the truck in the fading light of a winter's day.

The Purple Plastic Worm

...

NOTHING IN NATURE LOOKS LIKE A NINE-INCH-LONG PURPLE plastic worm. It doesn't matter. The purple plastic worm is one of our civilization's triumphs, sort of like discovering that tomatoes are not poisonous and that consuming the byproducts of decomposing fruit and grain, in small doses, can bring a little cheer into life. During the tumbling generations of humankind, I suspect that desperation, accidents, and blind evolutionary processes probably have contributed more to our quality of life, if not our very survival, than have purposeful endeavors. But regardless, the world has the purple plastic worm, and I'm happy about that. I will not question whether or not there was reason applied during its creation.

I have absolutely no idea why a largemouth bass wants to bite a purple plastic worm. Maybe it's because it's something new and different, out there creeping along the bottom of a pond, plowing a shallow furrow in the ooze. It's out there, in the domain of the bass, causing a small ruckus in an otherwise tranquil world, but ever so slight . . .

That may be the point. It is an irritant, sort of like a dripping faucet in the bathroom when you're trying to go to sleep. You quietly and calmly go to the thing and gently, sometimes firmly, take care of the situation. Or, perhaps, in another state of mind, you try to ignore the dripping for a while, covering your head with pillows, and then finally jump out of bed in a rage, rip the sink off the wall, and then have to go outside and shut off the water to the house before the new carpet is ruined. Bass treat purple plastic worms both ways.

As for the color, I've tried many. But since childhood I've found that purple tends to out catch all other colors of plastic worms. I'm pretty sure than once the worm is more than a couple of feet below the surface of the water it doesn't look purple at all, but probably something closer to black. But I've tried black, and I'll catch two to three bass on purple for every one I catch on black. It doesn't make any sense to me. But then I'm not a bass. It might not make sense to a bass either . . . assuming that the bass in question is thinking about worms and their colors in some rational way.

If I want to have an exciting fishing trip, I don't fish with a plastic worm. It takes forever and a coon's age to fish the things. Perhaps that's the point. If you're in a hurry or nervous, or pumped up with spit and vinegar, fishing with a plastic worm will make you go mad and bite yourself. To thoroughly fish a one-acre pond with a plastic worm could (and should) take most of a day. You can fish the same pond with a crank bait in about fifteen minutes.

If you don't really care whether or not you catch fish, but the possibility of doing so seems appealing (if by chance it were to occur), and you just want to be off by yourself outside, then sitting in a boat with a purple plastic worm on the end of your fishing line can be the perfect enterprise. It is up to you whether or not you actually put the worm in the water. I know some people who do and some who don't. Those who don't just tie on a worm, lay the rod down, and sit in the boat or on the pond bank staring at the water. I understand. I also know people who collect grass seed as a hobby.

There are many ways to rig and fish a purple plastic worm. Most people thread the hook through one end, the big end. They think that's the head, but having studied worm behavior I know that's wrong. The little end is the worm's head. But what the heck. Perhaps a worm moving in reverse stimulates predatory response from a bass more than one seemingly moving boldly forward with caution tossed to the wind ... er ... the currents. Other worm fishermen have recently taken to hooking the plastic worm through the middle, then throwing it out into a likely spot and just letting it sit there. I prefer a moving worm and so I thread mine through the "head" end. Sometimes I use a weight and sometimes I don't.

Several years ago people used hooks that had lead heads molded directly onto the hook. These hooks could be rigged under the worm and back up through the worm's body in a way to make the worm almost weedless and snag proof. They caught fish, but then fishermen began to think that the fish could feel the extra weight and would drop the bait. I personally don't think this mattered because how could a fish know what a purple plastic worm was in the first place and whether or not such a critter is supposed to have a heavy head (I mean "tail"). You see, this stuff can get pretty confusing if you start to think about it ... which you really shouldn't. Thinking about fishing a purple plastic worm defeats the purpose. When fishing a plastic worm, you are not supposed to think—at least not about catching fish anyway.

Another way to rig a worm is to have a small lead weight (they come in different sizes) with a hole through the middle. They look like blunt cones or are oblong. The thought is that by threading your line through the weight, when the fish picks up the worm, the line will slip through the weight and the fish won't feel the weight. Frankly, I think this is nonsense because that assumes that the fish is going to move only in one direction, directly away from the weight, not at an angle. If the fish moves away in any of the other 359 degrees possible from the weight, there will be drag. Does that matter? Perhaps stuff like that matters to anglers, but it doesn't seem to matter to the fish. The fish just pick up the strange creature that's invaded their turf and carry it off to kill and perhaps eat.

I tend to fish using this slip sinker technique, but it's really just because I did it once. I get into ruts, and the idea of any change at all when I'm fishing is repugnant to me. I don't experiment. I fish. Others may catch more fish than I do, but few come home from a fishing trip with a greater sense of satisfaction for having spent the day well. It might be helpful to elaborate via example.

The grass was happily growing in my lawn . . . lush and soft under the bare feet of small children frolicking about the place. The air was thick and humid. Hummingbirds hovered around the nectar feeder that was hanging near the daylilies. My two hunting dogs were stretched out in dirt holes they'd scratched in the shade of a fig tree. My wife was hanging clothes on a line to freshen as they dried. Billowing clouds were beginning to build on the distant horizon. Throughout the neighborhood there was dull murmuring and humming as desperate men (murmuring) and their machines (humming) whacked at their grass.

I decided I'd let my grass remain happy for another day, and perhaps more, because rain was forecast for the next couple of days. A couple of my neighbors, with sweat dripping from their beaded brows, saw me loading my fishing equipment, walked over to me, and said it was the last chance to cut grass before the rain. I said it was the last chance to go fishing before the rain and crawled into my pickup truck.

I drove out to my farm and across the pasture to where I have a little boat parked on the edge of a pond. I loaded two stiff worming rods, a small tackle box, and a little cooler, within which rested two cans of beer on ice. Checking carefully to be sure there were no snakes under my boat, I set sail to the middle of my one-acre pond and dropped anchor. I rigged a slip sinker, tied on a new hook, threaded a worm through the *tail*, and made my first cast.

The line on the reel immediately snarled and tangled. Out in the pond, perhaps sixty feet from my boat, there was a plop as my purple plastic worm hit the water and started sinking. I'd forgotten to adjust the tension on the reel to the weight of the lure. The result was that the reel's spool spun faster than the lure could pull the line off of the spool. There before me, in my hands, was the classic "bird's nest."

I sat there for a couple of minutes looking at it. There was no discernable pattern to this masterpiece. I'd like to say that it was a once in a lifetime accomplishment, but over the years as an angler, I've achieved this level of perfection many times. Untangling the mess was going to take some time . . . a lot of time. I had another rod with me, but there is such a thing as honor.

Honor, however, does not necessarily need to be addressed immediately. The small cooler on the bottom of the boat beckoned me come hither. It was just the other side of midafternoon . . . close enough to four o'clock, and the early summer sun was well into generating a real scorcher of a day. Cicadas were tuning up down in the woods below my pond. Their humming resonated through the thick air. I could feel it penetrate into my bones. The water was glassy smooth, other than the occasional swirl of small fish in the shallows as they snapped at wayward grasshoppers.

A shadow passed overhead as a great blue heron drifted in. It landed over where the fish were swirling. When it landed it stood very still, absolutely motionless, in the shallow water. It obviously understood, as did I, that this wasn't a day to rush anything. And it was especially not a day for a fisherman to rush into fixing a backlash on a bait-casting reel.

So, I put down the rod and reached for that cooler. Inside was my treasure of cold drinks. I chose one and, after popping the top to open it, felt the coolness of its sweat in my hands as water condensed on the surface of the can. I rubbed that cool water across my face, then took a long drink.

The reel with the "bird's nest" was resting on the boat seat beside me in all its glory. It was as if it knew that I was a captive—that I had no choice. At some point I'd either get the line untangled or I'd have to cut it off the reel's spool and put on fresh line. My purple plastic worm was still on the bottom of the pond.

I took about five minutes to finish my drink, then spent nearly twenty minutes working on that backlash. I'd find little loops of line and gently tug, loosening the intertwined grip of other loops, gaining a few inches of free line at a time, until I had it all free of the reel and the line was freely floating in the water beside the boat.

The heron didn't seem amused but did show polite interest. It stayed put until I was ready to reel in the line, then, with a squawk from one end and a salute from the other, lifted off and left me in solitude.

Pinching the line between thumb and forefinger so that tangles wouldn't pass back into the reel, I started retrieving the loose line from the water. It came wonderfully and smoothly back onto the reel's spool. I kept reeling until the line between the tip of the rod and my lure out on the bottom of the pond was straight.

Lowering the tip of the rod to the pond's surface, I gradually lifted it, ever so slowly, "crawling" the worm across the bottom. The worm had not moved more than five or six inches before there was a tapping that sent its messages all the way up from the worm, through the line, down the rod, and into my heart. Quickly I lowered the rod's tip again and watched as the line began to move and then to tighten. When the line was straight, I jerked the rod back as hard as I could, and whatever it was on the other end jerked back equally as hard.

The rod bent double and the line sang as it sliced the water. I could tell that it was a good fish. Then I saw the line start to come toward the surface. The fish was going to jump. I readied myself, knowing that when it cleared the water I'd only have a split second to pull the fish off balance before it shook its head, trying to dislodge the hook from its mouth.

Up it came. It was not just a good fish—it was a huge fish (for my pond), perhaps seven or eight pounds. As truly big fish are prone to do, it did not completely clear the water when it came up. It only came half way out, just enough so that I could see its monstrous mouth and flapping gill covers, just enough to get the perfect leverage, with over half of its body still in the water, for sending my purple plastic worm flying through space . . . which it did.

I was left with a slack line and a mind full of images. It was a tremendous fish and a great experience. I would have loved to have brought it to the boat and, in fact, have done so previously. "Eddie Joe" and I are old friends. We've tangled several times over the years. He usually wins these events, but from time to time I win. Afterwards, we shake hands. He goes back into the pond and I keep on fishing. He has three buddies almost as big as he is living with him in the pond. They all have names and histories.

This particular encounter with Eddie Joe confirmed what I've learned through the ages: the slower you fish a purple plastic worm, the better. My worm that day had been resting completely stationary for over twenty minutes as I worked on untangling my line. That bass knew it was there from the beginning. Neither the bass nor I were in any sort of rush. The time spent working on the line really wasn't much more time than I'd have spent just working the worm back to me had that first cast been a good one. Fish are not dumb. They know that worms, even purple ones, crawl . . . slowly.

Fishing a plastic worm is for the contemplative angler. The angler can fish without interrupting his train of thought. When I fish with a plastic worm I tend to be more sensitive to the world around me. I watch the turtles and dragonflies. I pay attention to the orange flowers on trumpet vines that grow among the willows on my pond's islands. I look deeply into the water and adjust my focus. When I do this I can actually see the tiny white specks of plankton. The biggest ones are about the size of a pin's head. But most are smaller. I imagine their world, adrift in the "sea" of my pond. If I stare down into the depths long enough, I enter into a different realm of transcendental being. A worm fisherman probes deeply. I have to be careful not to fall out of the boat.

I made a dozen or so casts during a thirty-minute period. Then I cast to the edge of a downed treetop beside one of my pond's islands. It's where I stand during the winter when I'm hunting ducks. As slowly as I could I worked the worm over and around branches, trying not to get the hook hung on anything. I had the hook embedded in the worm in a way to make it "weedless." But, regardless, if I fished too quickly the hook could still snag on things. So, when I felt the worm going over a branch, just as soon as it cleared the branch I'd give it slack line and let it fall back down into deeper water. I did this twice and then felt a series of small bumps indicating that a fish had intercepted the worm during the last free fall.

Again I watched as the line began to straighten. I readied myself, then slammed back with all my force, trying to bring the point of the hook out from the protective shield of the plastic worm's body and into the flesh of the fish's mouth. I was successful and the hook found its mark. The fish nearly jerked the rod from my hands. I held on and reeled like the dickens, trying to get that bass away from the treetop. It bore down toward deeper water out in the middle of the pond, away from snags and other cover that could be used to break off. Once it was out in the open water I knew that I had it. The runs became shorter and shorter and then, finally, I was able to bring the fish alongside the boat. I grabbed it by its lower jaw and swung it into the boat. It weighed about two pounds. I unhooked it and then gently released it back into the pond. I typically don't keep bass from my pond that weigh more than two pounds. The smaller fish are better eating and I want the larger fish, like Eddie Joe and his buddies, to just keep on growing . . .

I fished another hour without so much as a nibble. That's the way it can be sometimes when fishing a plastic worm. And it didn't matter—catching more fish, that is. What *did* matter was that I was feeling pretty good about things in general. I'd hooked two fine fish and landed and released one of them. I was pleased to know that Eddie Joe was still alive and active in my pond. The sky and the sun and the water and all the other things like bugs and birds and beer and the quiet had worked their magic on me.

It's hard for such treasures to touch your heart—and perhaps even you soul—when you focus too intently on catching fish, casting and reeling, casting and reeling, working a lure quickly, and whipping the water to a froth. Aren't fish, after all, mostly just an excuse to be there? With a sigh, however, I must admit that it took me over half a century of fishing to figure this out.

That afternoon out on my pond I had not focused on catching fish. I'd simply focused on fishing. It is the purple plastic worm that has, through the years, helped me understand the difference.

Old Barns

...

AT A VERY EARLY AGE I LEARNED ABOUT MAGNETS. PRIOR TO entering the pastoral ministry, my father was a botanist and agricultural research scientist. He loved science and shared that love with me until I caught the fever. He'd haul me to natural history museums, take me fishing, and let me accompany him when he'd go to work helping people control unwanted vegetation in ponds and community lakes across the southeastern United States. For Christmas and on birthdays I'd open presents to find magnifying glasses and "science" sets full of toy microscopes, dissecting equipment, and chemicals to make "reactions" (mostly stuff that bubbled in water and changed colors). Invariably, there would be some sort of magnet and a package of tiny steel fibers that you could pull with it. You were supposed to put the fibers on a piece of paper and then bring the magnet up under the paper to see how the fibers distributed themselves. But I would usually make a mess and then end up having to clean up by moving my magnet around on the floor, picking up the fibers so they wouldn't stick in peoples feet as they walked barefooted across the kitchen floor. The result of this was that my magnets usually had a fuzz of fibers on them regardless of how much I tried to clean them. I would also get old bolts and nails and feel the pull of the magnet.

About this time I learned to read, and the world opened to me. My senses were flooded by the world around me. My mind was flooded by the world of words. Together they merged and flooded my heart. Although I hadn't yet learned the meaning of metaphor, I experienced it. I discovered other "magnets" that pulled me relentlessly closer into their realm. Mornings full of birdsong, creeks, drippy hollows, brushy fencerows, old ponds, and sunsets were (and still are) some of the more powerful magnets that channeled my internal forces and gave me direction.

During those early formative years, my father's pastorates were in rural north-central Kentucky. I'd tag along as he called on his parishioners. Most lived out in the country and most owned or rented small farms. After greetings we'd typically be invited inside the house. I'd sit and fidget in the parlor, living room, or kitchen until released by my father with the words: "Don, why don't you run along outside and play? I'll call you when I'm ready to go." And then there might be a word or two from the parishioner about staying out of the pasture with the bull, or not to climb into the pen with the sow and her newborn pigs, or to beware of a certain rooster and if chased to stand my ground, not run—or else I'd get flogged by the rooster. The prospects of adventuring exploded in my soul and I'd be gone. I'd rush outside feeling the sweetness of absolute freedom, but really I wasn't free because there would almost always be the strongest magnet that ever existed in the world pulling me to it: an old barn.

These days it seems that barns in the South, at least those with character, are increasingly rare. Most barns now tend to be of the prefabricated metal variety. They serve their purposes, certainly, but sadly that's about it. They also tend to be closed up and locked—testimony to changing social mores. But back when I was a kid, barns were magical places, wide open and absolutely accessible. They were constructed of timbers and boards. I can't remember any of them being painted. If they had once upon a time received paint, you couldn't tell it. Rather, they were gray and weathered and seasoned by the passages of time.

I entered barns as I would caves. They were full of shadow, mystery, ghosts and spirits. They had strange, dank odors. The wind would whisper through the cracks. Sunlight would filter in through those same cracks. The timbers would creak and pop. There would be quiet rustlings as birds and small critters shifted position. Chickens would purr and cluck. Sometimes there would be the heavier movement of large animals: cattle or horses or mules. There was a sense of peace in old barns . . . and security. I recall that when out playing or working, if a storm came up, people didn't run to the house to get out of it. Rather they ran to the barn. I don't know why this was, but somehow the barn seemed much more inviting. Perhaps it was that the barn offered the necessary shelter while simultaneously providing us a ringside place to witness nature's power lash the earth.

These old barns oozed history and culture. Many had been around since the early 1900s, and some dated back to the mid 1800s. There were things in those barns that had been around for a very long time. It was not unusual to find old tools, farm implements, and harnesses that spoke clear messages about a time when muscle was more important than fuel. Some of the leather would be old and cracked, but amazingly I'd find some that still received loving care. Tools would have wooden handles slick and smooth and beautifully finished by human sweat. Metal would have patina so rich and thick that rust was impossible. Some of the brass, particularly on harnesses, was absolutely beautiful. Most things that I encountered in the barns had obvious places where they belonged. I rarely encountered clutter or piles of discarded junk. For the most part there was beautiful yet unique order in the barns. When I entered, I sensed this order. It was akin to the order that exists in a good camp. I loved it. The magnet drew me ever deeper into its realm.

There were basically two kinds of barns in the part of Kentucky where I lived my early years. There were barns for livestock, tools, and equipment, and there were barns for tobacco. The former tended also to have haylofts. The tobacco barns typically just had rafters and perhaps places for tractors and wagons to park. I prowled them all.

I was fairly small as a boy and that was a treasured asset. I could squeeze through holes and climb on rafters with swiftness and ease. I wasn't afraid to burrow deeply into stacks of hay bales. Nor was I afraid to climb to the ultimate heights of rafters. I'd been taught to respect other people's property so generally left things where I found them. But I'd handle them, climb on them, and try to figure out how things worked and what they were for. I was careful around sharp-edged tools. I never tried to start machines. But, if there was a horse around I'd bridle it and ride it. If I couldn't find a bridle, I'd construct one from baling twine or just ride by steering with the horse's mane. I didn't bother with saddles.

It seemed to me that most horses like small boys. Horses seem also to capture the same sense of adventure that the boy has when the boy approaches the horse. I wasn't afraid of horses and horses sensed this. They'd come to me and I'd pet them and then the next thing they knew I was on top and we'd be off, riding around the barn's perimeter or out across pastures. Sometimes a horse would get a little frisky and I'd fall off. Sometimes when I'd fall it would knock the breath out of me. Other than a few bruises and scratches, I was never hurt. Rarely, after falling off, would the horse I'd been riding leave me. Rather, most would come back to check on me, push me with their muzzle, and stand patiently as I recovered and climbed back onboard. They are very special animals and to this day we can whisper to each other. There's telepathy, an unspoken mind meld that joins us.

During these same years I also fell in love with pigeons. I'd read about them in Boy Scout magazines and longed to have some. I would watch them fly in those graceful wheeling flocks around barns and grain storage silos. I dreamed of taking my pigeons far away and turning them loose to "home" back to their loft. But, being the son of a preacher and elementary school teacher, with a weekly allowance of fifty cents (supplemented by selling drink bottles back to grocery stores for two cents apiece), I didn't have money to buy the fine pigeons advertised in magazines. I had to make do with what pigeons I could get my hands on—literally.

Catching pigeons as a small boy was almost impossible except during a very special time of year. During late summer and early fall tobacco would be harvested. The stalks would be speared onto long, split sticks. The sticks of tobacco would be hung on the rafters of tobacco barns until the leaves cured. The rafters went to the very inside top of the barns and the tobacco sticks would be so thick that a small boy could work his way unseen right to the top . . . where the pigeons lurked. With great care and stealth I'd work my way silently up to the top, hardly breathing, barely rustling the leaves, carefully peering through the hanging rows, tightly spaced, until I spied pigeons. Then, after coiling like some panther, I'd spring up into the flurry of wings, both hands desperately trying to catch a pigeon in flight. I was so lightweight that I didn't worry about breaking the tobacco sticks and falling to the ground. I'd actually plan on falling, just to the first layer of tobacco sticks. Sometimes, miraculously, as the sticks arrested my fall, I'd be laying on my back with a very much alive pigeon in my hands! The pigeons I'd catch were treasures beyond treasure. I'd tuck the live bird inside my shirt and button up tightly. Then I'd climb down through the tiers of tobacco sticks and transport my prize to the pigeon coop I'd constructed on my back porch.

The pigeons tamed quickly and tended to hang around when I finally got up the courage to let them fly around the house. They'd come back to the coop and walk around my feet as I'd feed them. But they would not let me catch them when they were out like that. They had to be inside the coop for me to get my hands on them.

I was convinced that they were "sure enough" homing pigeons of the "racer" variety because I could get on my bicycle and take them to the far side of the small town where we lived, release them, and they'd be back at their coop before I could get back on my bicycle. The reality was that they were just barn pigeons . . . the coop was probably no more than half a mile from the release point.

I was ten years old when my father received a call to come home, to serve as pastor of a church back in the Deep South, the land and the heritage that stroked his soul. I sensed his excitement but didn't understand it. The move meant that my pigeon days were over, but not my love and affinity for old barns. The force of that magnet was as strong as ever.

Later in life, when I became a professional biologist, I learned about imprinting and how it happens to critters at critical times in early life. And that's exactly what happened to me following our move. I imprinted on everything "Southern": the climate, the hills and creeks and bottoms, the lakes, tupelo and cypress swamps, the hunting and fishing, and the prevailing undercurrent of independence, self reliance, community and—most particularly—the region's propensity for eccentricity . . .

It is said that people in the Deep South do not step to the beat of a different drummer. Rather, they have never heard the rhythm section at all. There were rain makers during droughts who drove pickup trucks equipped with boilers that sent special chemicals into clouds to seed them. There were politicians who garnered votes planting "farkleberry" bushes alongside state highways. Although there was sophistication in the major cities, with symphonies, theater, and oratory, the veneer was pretty thin. The true grain of life close to the earth—life framed in pioneer spirit—was only a scratch away.

And so it was that although our home was on the outskirts of a metropolitan zone, I was only minutes away from lakes where I could fish, swim, and prowl. There were woods equally near and for all practical purposes I lived in them. If I rambled deep into these woods, I'd link up with a fabulous creek full of bullhead catfish and groves of big oak and hickory trees virtually dripping with fox squirrels.

When I turned eleven years old, I was given a single-shot .22 rifle. When I turned twelve, I was given a single-shot .410 shotgun. After school and on weekends, depending on the season, I'd either be on the lake down at the end of the road, paddling around in some old boat, or rambling through the woods with gun in hand. Nobody back then was in the least concerned about boys walking down the street with a gun, heading for the woods, or about boys shoving off in a "borrowed" boat to go fishing. We were safe. We were respectful of property, including that which we occasionally borrowed for our adventuring. I was fortunate to live in a community that was a real community in every sense of the world. Children were reared as a corporate endeavor.

Given the opportunity, boys tend to grow larger in spirit as well as body. When that started happening rapidly during my early high school years—when I was fourteen or fifteen years old and adding about an inch a month to my height—the woods and waters near my home, although still treasures, simply were not big enough to satisfy my wanderlust. The problem, however, was that I was not old enough to drive a car alone. The only way for me to get to the wilder places was for somebody to take me. I had a friend, Don Flynn, who suffered the same malady.

Our parents did not hunt and rarely fished. But they read our hearts and sensed our spiritual longings to be out in the wilds. They'd drive us to new places on the outskirts of town, drop us off, and let us ramble for a while as they waited back in the car. That didn't work. We loved them for the effort, but a couple of hours on a Sunday afternoon or an hour or so after school wasn't enough time to settle into any sort of hunt or any sort of fishing. There had to be another way. My father figured it out and set the stage.

In my father's church was an elderly couple, Dale and Ester Cartmell, who lived in a log cabin about fifteen miles outside of town. My father talked with them and explained the issues and the challenges. The Cartmells quickly captured the spirit of conspiracy. They said they would be very happy to have boys again on their farm, around their home, and prowling around the place with fishing poles and guns. They had children, but their children were already grown and gone. So, in fairly short order, we were informally adopted. We became their boys and they became much-loved uncle and aunt.

The farm had about fifty acres of woods, pasture, and hills through which ran a substantial creek. The creek ran clear and occasionally tucked up against a bluff. There were catfish, bass, and bream in the creek; gray squirrels and, occasionally, fox squirrels were thick in the woods. During late winter there would even be a few ducks on the creek.

These were the years before deer and turkey were common in the region. We never really thought about them and never saw any sign. But it didn't matter. Squirrels and wood ducks commanded our attention during hunting season, bullheads and bass during fishing season. Heaven couldn't possibly be finer.

I don't understand why this small farm seemed wilder and bigger to us than the hundreds of acres of oak forest near our homes, but it did. Maybe it was the drive, the distance out of town, that gave it such a remote feeling. Maybe it was the pioneer spirit of the Cartmell's cabin and how they lived on the land. They had electricity but heated with a wood stove. Their water came from a well. They milked cows, killed hogs, had a garden, churned butter, made jellies, baked bread, and welcomed us when we showed up. And they gave us a very special gift. We were given full access to their old barn.

This was the key that unlocked the wilder world to us. It was tucked off to the side of the cabin, perhaps fifty yards away and adjacent to a lane that led down to the creek. It was a working barn, a place where equipment, cattle, and hay were kept. There was plenty of room in it for two boys to "make camp," and it was far enough away from the cabin that two boys could talk and "cut up" all night long without disturbing our sleeping hosts.

So, we'd be hauled out to Cartmell's farm by our parents on Friday afternoons after school and dumped on the front porch of the cabin. We would not be picked up until late Saturday afternoon or early evening. There would be fresh cookies waiting for us when we arrived, and sometimes dinner. But mostly we brought our own food and a gallon jug of milk to drink. We were forbidden to have a fire or a lantern because the barn was a good one and as dry as tinder inside. The planking was tight and the roof was good. The cold wind could howl and the rain and sleet could rip and tear, but we'd be snug and warm in our nests up in the hayloft.

Don and I would lay there in our sleeping bags, with our guns and our food and our gallon of milk close at hand, talking quietly, unknowingly engaged in lifelong bonding as brothers more than friends. We'd hear the cattle stirring and the rustling of mice. On still nights, beyond the barn, we could hear owls and, occasionally, the call of snow geese as they passed overhead.

The call of the geese would sometimes stir the restlessness in our souls so much that we'd sacrifice the warmth of our sleeping bags and go outside just to look up, hoping to see the geese. But they were impossible to see in the dark and infinitely deep sky. What we encountered on these forays beyond the barn on winter nights was more powerful, however, than any geese. The sky sometimes would be incredibly clear. On such nights the stars would seem to hang overhead so close that we could imagine just reaching up and picking them, if only we had arms just a little longer. So we'd reach out to them with the only other thing that stood a chance of making the encounter ... our dreams of a wilder way. We'd stand out under that canopy, looking, listening, feeling the closeness of brotherhood, feeling the awesome reality of God (and sometimes even talking about it), and stroking the spirit of adventure that swelled within our youthful breasts. The starlight would sparkle on the frost that covered the grass beneath our feet. There would be moon shadows that oozed mystery. We were beyond the reach of civilization's noise ... beyond the glow of its lights. There was a quietness that surrounded us. It merged with a growing quietness within us. We'd shiver a little, but it wasn't just because of the chill in the air.

That old barn on Cartmell's farm was certainly a magnet that drew us back to it time and time again. We loved that old barn. In some ways I think we loved it as much if not more than the wild lands that surrounded it. It was more than a magnet, however.

It was the catalyst that opened a way into worlds we'd otherwise only imagined. We realized that without that barn we wouldn't have access to the farm for hunting and fishing. With the barn we were flooded by blessings of outdoor adventure in myriad forms.

We were just boys . . . boys still too young to drive, and yet boys alone with guns, governed by the admonition that we were, in no uncertain terms, accountable for how we behaved, accountable for what we did and how we did it. We understood this. We understood also that we were accountable for our own lives . . . not just in terms of health and safety as we hunted and fished out there on that land, but life expressed in the full extent of its meaning—beyond the realms of sportsmen, beyond the realms of boyhood. We did not betray that trust.

When I think back across the years about Cartmell's barn and all of the other old barns that have touched my life, I do so with a sense of reverence for them. They are sacred places to me. The more I think about them, the more my feelings about old barns seem to meld with the feelings I have for the churches that have framed my sojourn.

They are good feelings, so I shut my eyes, breathe deeply, and let my thoughts flow freely. In doing so, I begin to envision old barns, particularly those of my youth, scattered all along the trail of an ethereal pilgrimage. I step out on that trail. I can feel the movement of spirits on it and . . . in the stillness I am enveloped by the presence of God . . . a presence that floods me to the core of my being.

My reflections move ever deeper. They invoke a state of communion that is as moving as any heralded by bread or wine. It flows from the deepest well of memories, from beyond the realm of the oversoul: the tart odor of curing tobacco hanging on rafters, the beating of a pigeon's heart next to my own under my shirt, the slick surfaces of old tools, the mellow glow of fine leather, the warmth of a hayloft on a winter's night, the greater warmth of friendship in the loft, shared in conversation and in silence, the creaking boards . . . the rustlings of life within and beyond.

Such are the sacraments of old barns. We safeguard them in our memories. We hold them in our hearts.

To Dance with a Kindred Bird

...

THERE IS A SPECIAL CHARM OUT YONDER IN THE WILDS THAT can only be found in the South's damper places. They are not wetlands, but neither are they dry. A little mud may accumulate on your boots, but rarely will you feel it sucking at your feet. You'll rarely have to slosh or muck your way to adventure. If you roll a log you're apt to find a salamander, and if you scratch the ground there will be earthworms.

These damper places drain well. Ferns adorn the banks of swales and on the higher spots there will be patches of moss. When the temperature and humidity are within the correct multivariate dimensions, mushrooms will poke their heads out from under the leaf litter. On clear nights, under the stars, fairies likely come to these places to dance on the moss and sit on the mushrooms. The shadows are deep and the mystery even deeper, particularly after midnight. These places can be just a little bit spooky.

During spring, frog calls of all sorts drift in the night air through these places, melding their symphony with the clear notes of whip-poor-wills and chuck-will's-widows. Coyotes and owls herald the coming of dawn.

In summer and early autumn these woods provide any and all who venture within with a cool and shady refuge from the sun, but not from mosquitoes. They will test resolve for cool solace without mercy. It is rarely windy in these woods because the trees are spaced just right to catch the breezes and stop them. In fact, these woods are typically so still that it's almost like being in a cathedral on a Monday morning.

In late autumn, after a few light frosts have brushed the Mississippi landscape with their magic and the trees are on fire with color and beginning to drop their leaves, and just before cold weather settles in, a wave of solitary migrant sojourners begins to flutter in from the North over the course of a few special nights, settling quietly into the Deep South's damper woodlands. Their arrival sets the stage for another sort of dance that has nothing at all to do with fairies. It is a dance known primarily to a few eccentric woods ramblers who are one in spirit with those damper places and their denizens. More specifically, it is a hunter's dance, a dance that, for a few weeks each year, celebrates the most unpredictable, fleeting, and mysterious of all hunts in Mississippi . . . the hunt for woodcock.

This bird is as strange and eccentric as the hunters who pursue it—perhaps, it is the other way around. It is technically a shorebird but is rarely found on a shoreline. It prefers to be in damp woods with young (but not too young) hardwood trees, spaced closely (but not too closely) so that there is cover, but also enough shade in the summer to keep the ground fairly open. Woodcock like to feel the good earth under their bare feet. A damp woodland or even an old brushy field that has been lightly touched by fire can be perfect in this regard. Regardless, woodcock don't like windy places. For this reason, many woodcock hunters smoke old pipes. If you can't light your pipe, move on.

Unlike other shorebirds, the woodcock is a solitary creature. It does not flock. It is rather quiet and independent and is apparently not bound to any sort of social order. It doesn't move around much during the day, but rather just hunkers down in a good spot where it can take naps and watch the world around it. It is a courageous bird, however, and will hold tight to its spot, staring a bird dog right in the face, eyeball to eyeball, as a hunter walks up to it. So firmly resolved in courage is the woodcock that a hunter frequently is forced to kick one up into the air in order to get a "flush"—with the dog left trembling and slobbering as the hunter tries to mount the gun for a shot. (The hunter is also likely to be trembling and slobbering at this point.)

The woodcock feeds at night and is most active at dusk and dawn. Its large eyes are set toward the rear of the head, giving the woodcock a propensity to dwell more on the past than the present or future. It flutters almost vertically when first flushed. Once airborne and above all but the tallest treetops, it hesitates momentarily, finally decides where it wants to go, and then heads that way with determination . . . as if it knew its destination all along, which, of course, it didn't.

In these and other respects, woodcock hunters tend to reflect the personality traits of woodcock and share many of their values and life orientations. The only real difference between woodcock and woodcock hunters is that woodcock fly and eat earthworms. Woodcock hunters do neither (although I'm sure some try). Were it not for these differences, however, I suppose woodcock hunters might identify too much with woodcock and stop hunting and shooting the things. Thank God for the differences.

When I first bought my farm in Mississippi, before I'd linked with the rhythms of the place and developed a bit of perspective, I spent a lot of time sitting in deer stands just watching the woods around me. I was, after all, a stranger in the realm. I had not yet recognized the subtle differences that defined the various landscapes of the place. I had not yet developed a proper sense of scale or relativity. I tended to underestimate the deeper currents that swirled around me. I had little appreciation of transient and fickle micro-seasons that were nested within broader temporal scales that determine movements of wildlife, both resident and temporary. But I *knew* that I didn't know, and so I just sat in deer stands . . . watching, listening, waiting, thinking. I shot a few deer during this apprenticeship, but it wasn't the deer that were my treasures, wonderful though they were. Rather, it was the hours spent in stillness, watching . . . feeling, that were my real treasures.

I had to wait . . . wait for the place to reveal itself to me. A few years passed. Although I didn't know it at the time, I was becoming a woodcock hunter. It was the sitting, the waiting, the listening, and the watching that made the difference. I had to connect with the rhythms of the place. I knew that I couldn't find what I was searching for by rambling around, at least not at first.

First and foremost, I had to learn how to move and meld on a smaller scale than I was used to. I'd come to Mississippi from big places, huge places, open places, deserts, jungles, mountain ranges, tundra, taiga, wilderness in the most absolute sense of the word. Now, I was on fifty acres five miles south of a college town in the Deep South. It was a good fifty acres and in the right place, but still it was "only" fifty acres. The important thing, however, was that it was mine. I'd bought it. I had title to it. I could develop a deep and personal relationship with it without worrying about somebody else busting into my realm.

Regardless, the adjustment still took time . . . a lot of time . . . years. But with the years I began to see, to know, to understand, to sense meaning. And when I did, I began to encounter woodcock.

The first woodcock I saw on my farm was on the ground, in the shadows at dusk, about fifteen yards from where I was sitting in a deer stand one deep November afternoon. I'd seen movement down on the ground and at first thought it was a squirrel or maybe a bird like a brown thrasher. But then I recognized the round, plump body of the woodcock, its head held tight to its shoulders, and its long beak. It was probing the ground for earthworms along the edge of a damp swale beneath some water oaks. I watched it until darkness swallowed both of us.

I was happy about seeing that woodcock but chalked it up as a minor attribute of the farm. I also had quail on the farm, in fact, three coveys. But I didn't have a bird dog and I didn't harass them. As a hunter my focus during those formative years was deer, ducks, squirrels, and an occasional rabbit. Fifty acres in Mississippi can provide a man with that sort of hunting quite nicely.

My second woodcock encounter on the farm was early on a bright morning of an extremely cold day in January. I was rambling across a hill covered with pines . . . looking for deer, but not seriously. I'd already put three in the freezer that season. Mostly, I just wanted to be out and about, enjoying the day, connecting with the land. I had a rifle with me, not a shotgun. The ground was frozen elsewhere on the farm but under the pines it was still soft. The pines also stopped the gentle wind that drifted on and off across the hill. In the sunshine there among the pines it actually felt sort of warm. I paused to enjoy the warmth and the absence of wind.

When I paused, however, a woodcock jumped up in front of me, flew about six feet, landed, and stood on the trail I'd just walked on, looking at me with those huge dark and liquid eyes. I advanced slowly toward the bird. It walked away. I advanced more and it walked more. It didn't want to fly. It was too cold to fly. Eventually, it walked away and hid down in some grass among those pines. I remember, however, how it stopped and looked at me before it went into the shelter of the grass, as if making an assessment of what I was and what my intentions might be. Then it called "Peert" and disappeared. Absolutely a class act. Afterwards, as I looked around my feet, I saw small, round holes in the ground where the woodcock had been probing for earthworms. I'd never have guessed that earthworms would have been up there in the earth under the pines on a cold January morning. But the woodcock knew.

I started paying serious attention to woodcock after that encounter. Occasionally I'd flush them as I hunted squirrels or when I walked to or from deer stands. During duck season I'd see them as they flew over me just before shooting time. When they came over in the first gray light of day, they looked huge, and almost invariably I'd raise my gun thinking they were wood ducks. But soon I learned that the wood ducks don't come to my duck pond in the woods until after the woodcock have flown over me on their way to their day roost. I'd watch those woodcock land down in the damper woods below the pond, down among the green ash groves. Eventually, I got to where I wouldn't even load my gun on duck hunts until the woodcock had passed overhead. They were my signal that duck shooting was about to start.

More years passed. I had dogs, but my dogs were retrievers that I used for duck hunting. They were not bird dogs. One, however, would point, and from time to time after I finished a duck hunt and was rambling the farm with the dog on my way back to my truck, he'd point and I'd get a shot at quail. He'd also occasionally flush a woodcock. But I never got a shot at a woodcock.

Over the years I drifted from deer hunting more and more and focused ever more intently on ducks and squirrels. And the woodcock were always there . . . not many mind you, but still there. When I was out walking, particularly during December and January, I'd flush them from time to time. It seemed that they preferred a couple of places on my farm more than others, particularly the damper places, but generally speaking the entire farm started reveling itself to me as woodcock habitat. They'd be in different places at different times of the day and in yet different places depending on the weather. Although I didn't shoot at them, I thought about them . . . a lot.

My duck dogs got old and passed away. After their passing I got a puppy of a different breed, an American wirehaired pointing griffon. I named him Hank. I got Hank primarily as a retriever for my duck hunts, not realizing that he was, first and foremost, a pointing breed. But as a puppy he pointed everything—butterflies, sparrows, robins, cats, cockroaches, even squirrel skins tied on long strings to cane poles. Pointing was in his heart. He loved the duck hunts, but he adored bird (quail) hunts. The problem was that the quail on my farm had just sort of evaporated over the years. Friends of mine with land reported much the same thing. The quail were gone, at least huntable numbers of quail. So, to keep my puppy happy, I resorted to purchasing pen-raised, flight-conditioned quail. I'd release them on the farm, wait for a while, then get Hank and go hunt them. It was fake. It was artificial. And it was expensive. But it was fun and Hank loved it. I have to admit that I loved it too. Hank got to find the birds and point them. I got to walk with him, work the points, flush, and shoot.

Then one autumn day when it was so still that I could hear robins turning leaves looking for bugs and worms, a day when the sun was casting a golden glow over my farm and my heart was bursting with happiness just because I was out there in the middle of it all, Hank came down on a point down in the damp woods along my largest creek. This area along the creek encompasses about five acres and has green ash saplings spaced just like alders will space in more northern states. Here and there are a few large sycamores and water oaks. The ground is fairly clear, with little underbrush because of summer shading. Over the two decades I'd owned the farm, this part of the property had started to become one of my favorites. It has a certain mysterious feel to it. I like the way the terrain flows. I enjoy the deep earth smells. There are ferns and moss scattered about. And the soil is the best of Mississippi's prairie soil. It is just a little strip of that good prairie soil, but in it there is a richness like no other on the farm. And in it there are earthworms. It is absolutely earthworm territory and, subsequently, it is absolutely woodcock habitat.

I walked up to Hank and he held his point like a champ. The place seemed too wet for quail and I knew that the ones I'd released earlier that day were in a different part of the farm. So I looked carefully on the ground in front of Hank. I probably should not have done that because a bird hunter should always look out ahead, not at the ground. But I looked at the ground anyway. Finally, I saw the bird . . . and it was a woodcock.

When I saw that bird I just about came unglued. I was as happy as a kid on a Christmas morning who's just seen the electric train he'd been dreaming about now set up under the tree. I'd never shot a woodcock. I'd never shot *at* a woodcock. But it was about to happen. All the stories I'd read as a child about people hunting woodcock in the northern states came flooding into my mind. I was right there with them, with my dog and my fine double-barreled shotgun, there in the autumn woods . . .

The woodcock was so still. Hank was etched in stone. My heart was about to come out of my chest. I breathed deeply and switched my vision from the woodcock on the ground to the woods in front of me. I stepped forward. Then I took another step, just past the dog, and suddenly there were wings fluttering and the woodcock went rocketing vertically in front of me. Instinct took over and I shot just as it topped the young ash trees. Miracle of all miracles—that woodcock folded and came back to earth.

Hank was immediately on that woodcock, picked it up, and brought it to my hand. Hardly a feather was ruffled. The stripes across the head, the wonderful orange-brown feathers along its sides, the beautiful patterns of brown and chocolate on wings and back—it all sent me soaring. Here I was, a man over fifty years old with my first woodcock. I suddenly was twelve years old again, holding my first dove, walking to my first buck on the ground, retrieving my first wood duck from a creek at dawn.

I held that wonderful bird in my hands, looking at it, feeling it, touching its long beak, and marveling at the soft tip of the beak that it uses to catch worms. I looked at its shorebird feet and at its round and fluffy wings. It was everything I had ever hoped for in wing shooting and I'd done it on my own land, on my little Mississippi farm with a fabulous dog that made the entire event perfect . . . and a white beard on my chin to remind me that if you keep a dream long enough, it just might come true.

Shooting that woodcock opened a new world for me. I realized that this was definitely something that was possible, not only on my farm but elsewhere in the region of northeastern Mississippi where I live. Nobody hunted woodcock. Nobody had bird dogs anymore. Nobody cared except me. I cared.

And so I have become a woodcock hunter—in Mississippi. Since that first bird, Hank and I have taken many. They are sporadic and they are mysterious. They come, they go, they come again, then they disappear . . . only to return with their magic. But through their magic they pull me out into golden afternoons and onto gorgeous landscapes. They draw me to the mysterious damper places where spirits lurk. They link me to the earth, as do no other game birds. They challenge me with difficult shots as they flush straight up through the branches. I typically miss more than I hit. There's not a lot of shooting and yet there's enough.

When one of those golden afternoons is in the process of wrapping itself around my heart, filling my mind with a special sort of peace, and the mysteries of the damper places I'm exploring reach out and touch my soul—and especially when one or two woodcock are in my hunting coat pocket and my dog Hank is flowing like poetry in front of me through the green ash groves and the lingering smell of gun smoke is melding with the rich umber smells of late autumn woodlands—I will pause from time to time and quietly whisper to myself . . . in a sort of prayer, I suppose . . . that nothing on this earth could possibly make this old woods rambler any happier that to be engaged in the dance, this wonderful dance in the damper places with a very special, kindred bird.

The Tiger's Bridges

...

THE BUSHES DOWN BY THE WATER TREMBLED AND SWAYED IN the early morning shadows. As I slipped silently into those shadows, my heart was in my throat. My senses were on edge lest I be discovered by some wayward wanderer before I could close on the source of the disturbance. I could hear the blood rushing near my ears. A deep sense of aloneness enveloped me. There was a metallic taste in my mouth.

I pushed forward, toward the water . . . toward whatever it was that made those bushes move. I had no choice, no choice at all, because the night before I'd set the stage for what was about to happen. Now, I had to go the distance and, if necessary, do battle with the unknown beast—armed only with my bare hands. I wondered if I had the strength to do what had to be done. I was only twelve years old.

Hidden from view, among trees and grass, was a small boat that I'd used the previous evening, after dark, to create the situation I now faced. I pushed it out into the water, and as I did so, the bushes on the shoreline opposite from where I launched the boat thrashed violently, and there was a huge swirl in the water. The situation was terrifying. I was trembling but held steady on the course—paddling the small boat across the inky black water—absolutely alone in a world that became ever more intense with each passing moment. There was an unimaginable stillness . . . amplifying the sound of the moving bushes and the swirls in the water.

I went directly to the bushes, reached out, and grabbed the stout line that I'd tied to them. When I pulled on the line there was a tremendous force that pulled back and that nearly jerked me out of the boat and into the water. My hands were jerked from the lined and I fell back into the boat, landing on my back and bumping my head on one of the boat's seats. I wasn't hurt, but the shock of the fall flipped a switch of some sort. I was no longer the scared twelve-year-old boy. I was transformed into a warrior! Adrenaline surged through me as I reached for my boat paddle and went back to the bushes and to the line that was tied there.

Reaching out again, I grabbed the line and felt the power of my adversary. But this time I held on and fought—hard. Slowly and deliberately I worked my way along the line. The closer I got to the source of the fight, the more determined I became. Finally I was right on top of it. I pulled and the monster fought me furiously. I held on, as it came again and again to beat the side of my boat with its huge body. The boat dipped and swayed in the battle. I was soaking wet from the thrashing. Still I held the line, determined to win or die as a warrior.

The element of time evaporated as dawn crept across the water, chasing away the shadows and turning the water from black to gray. But I did not notice the dawn. I only noticed that now, when the monster came to the top, I could see clearly the hook that had us locked in battle.

I was afraid of that hook, and the others on the line, knowing that if somehow I became hooked, the monster would drag me down to my doom. But, having no net, I knew that the only way to ultimate victory would be to grab the giant by its mouth, that huge mouth that held the hook, and somehow drag the beast over the side of the boat.

I pulled ever harder and made my first grab. My hand went into the fish's mouth and grabbed the lower jaw. Immediately the monster bit down hard and plunged. I was nearly pulled out of the boat and was only saved by releasing my grip on the jaw.

As I jerked my hand back, the fish's teeth raked the skin from it. The hand was a bloody mess. But there was no time to deal with the pain or the bleeding. The deck and seats of the boat were splashed with blood as I threw myself back into the fight.

I pulled again and brought the fish closer once more. It thrashed and beat at the side of the boat as I held the line high with my left hand and plunged my injured right hand once again into the toothy mouth. Ignoring the pain, I held on with my right hand, dropped the line from my left hand, and then forced it into the fish's closed mouth. The fish's mouth was so tightly closed that I could barely get my left hand inside, but I had no choice. I pushed and pushed and, finally, was able to cram it inside. Then I gripped the lower jaw tightly with both hands. The fish twisted and tore at my flesh. I heaved as hard as I could with both of my thin, youthful arms, leveraging with my back and narrow shoulders, and finally brought the monster onboard.

As soon as it hit the bottom of the boat—the fish went crazy. The hook was still in its mouth, and the other hooks along the line were swinging wildly. I dug into the pocket of my wet jeans and pulled out my knife. As quickly as my wounded hands would let me, I opened the knife blade and cut the line near the fish's mouth. The rest of the trotline snapped back into the water. The fish stopped thrashing and then began to calm. I stroked it along its massive sides and it calmed even more. The danger of the hooks on the line was gone. The battle was over.

I'd just caught my very first flathead catfish, and it was huge. I didn't want to lift it, or even try, at least not out there in the boat, for fear of losing it. I knew it was secure right where it lay in the bottom of the boat, flat on its stomach, its huge head with those vicious jaws and beady eyes seemingly ready to attack again given the chance. I knew, however, that I needed to pull it to the center of the boat so that I could paddle back to the shore.

I didn't want to deal with the fish's head any more. My hands had suffered enough from that end. So, I tried to grab the base of the tail with both of my hands. But my hands were not large enough to reach around the base. It was just too big. Holding the tail and pushing with my feet I finally got the fish positioned in the boat where I wanted it.

When I got to the shore, I looped a rope tightly around the fish's tail and dragged the beast up onto the bank. I tethered the fish—on dry ground—to a small tree. Then I walked home to get my wagon because the fish was too big for me to carry. In fact, I could barely lift it. And, later, when I did lift it and was able to get its tail off the ground, the head was at my shoulders. I never weighed that fish, but now, reflecting back across the years, I think it probably weighed about thirty pounds, a respectable flathead catfish, but not particularly large by flathead catfish standards.

Something happens within the heart of a boy when he catches a fish like that. It isn't really imprinting. Rather, it seems that it helps the boy come to terms with a piece of life's framework. It helps him to recognize that there are large, strong, and potentially dangerous animals in the world that can and absolutely *will* fight you viciously, if necessary. It also helps the boy learn that if you fight back with determination, you just *might* win . . . might. And if the boy thinks about it much—and I did—he will grow to appreciate the fact that the things that fight back and that can hurt you also have their place in the scheme of things. Without them, the world wouldn't have the edge, the spice, the uncertainty, and the strange beauty that makes life the wonderful adventure that it is supposed to be.

When I caught that first flathead catfish as a young boy, I had no idea that this species of fish would ultimately define much of my career, or that it would become the foundation and framework of my professional identity. Nor did I realize the power of flathead catfish, the tigers of inland waters, as a bridge to bring people together for common cause, friendship, and fellowship. But this huge predator that prowls and hunts and fights in the murky, shadowy depths has done all of these things, and much more.

During my career as a professor of fisheries at Mississippi State University, I focused very hard on helping people understand how rivers work and on revealing humankind's linkages to these wonderful elements of God's creation. I discovered that people are fascinated by moving water, but when the waters are wild and, particularly, if those wild waters are turbid, they tend to be afraid. It is healthy to feel some fear regarding rivers because fear can be an important precursor to respect. However, and unfortunately, the fear of wild, turbid, moving water oftentimes inadvertently gives license (whether stated or not) to other people who are oriented toward doing bad things to rivers. That's not good for the critters that live in and with rivers. That's not good for us because rivers are part of the world we live in, have been for a long time, and, in my opinion, should be in the future that is unfolding ahead for us.

Rivers have defined much of who we are as a species. They have been our highways for adventure, exploration, conquest, and commerce. They have nurtured the earth to enhance our agricultural and forestry endeavors. They have given us water for myriad uses. They have been sources of food for us and also for the other life forms that share the planet with us. I'm not sure that we can live without them and, after a full career studying rivers and working with rivers, I'm not convinced that we know enough about them (or ourselves for that matter) to do the sorts of things that we have been doing to them—like ripping them apart with channelization, dredging the life from them with draglines, diverting them into places where they shouldn't be, cutting off their currents with dams, poisoning them with the residues of our "civilization," using them as our sewers, and sucking then dry for agricultural, municipal, and industrial uses. Slowly we are learning. Very slowly. But the steps on this journey of responsible stewardship fill my heart . . . because . . .

I am haunted by rivers . . . rivers past, river present, rivers future. I am drawn to them. They call to me. I can close my eyes and envision myself deep within their swirling currents, living among the denizens that prowl therein. My senses swell with the multidimensional forces that surround me. Those swirling currents set me free and within them I experience what it must be like to fly. There is beauty that transcends the limitations of my terrestrial being. I am at once in love with rivers and terrified by them. Their powers are relentless and in their midst I feel very, very small.

These fears are justified because rivers and the life forms that live in and around them can be dangerous, even for people who regularly move on and into them—people like me. But if you are thoughtful and careful and somewhat adventurous, they can be, and usually are, magic places. Having also worked extensively on large lakes and reservoirs, I can honestly say that the element of danger is about the same out on open water, just somewhat less obvious. And, in this regard, we think we've tamed a river when we put a dam on it. The river just laughs.

When working to enhance people's understanding and sense of responsibility toward rivers, you're wasting your time, at least in public arenas (where conservation has to happen), talking about water chemistry, physics, and ecosystem processes. People cannot or will not relate to such stuff. Nor is it fruitful to talk about bacteria, fungi, plankton, aquatic insects, worms, most crustaceans (crayfish excluded), or the myriad "lesser fishes" that inhabit these waters.

But when you invoke the realm of mystery into the conversation—and history and culture—and talk about big things that bite or can fight, and particularly if the critter is something that you can catch and eat, I've discovered, over the course of a lifetime in science and natural resources conservation efforts, that people will follow you without hesitation out into the deepest currents, figuratively and actually. There's something about wild rivers and the big, predacious fish that live in them that stirs our souls.

In this last regard, truly effective conservation of landscapes, including their associated waters, generally requires a focus on large predators. In the scientific and conservation arenas we call these animals "charismatic mega-fauna." So if you want to protect jungles, you absolutely must talk about tigers and jaguars. If you want to protect open savannas and similar dry lands, you talk about lions. If you want to protect wilderness areas in North America and Asia, you talk about bears and wolves. If you want to protect the oceans, you must talk about sharks. And . . . if you want to protect the rivers that grace the landscape in the southern United States, you must talk about flathead catfish.

If the big predator is doing OK, then the place where it lives is functioning as it should. The big predator is the ultimate reflection of how everything in its world is getting along over the long haul, over spatial expanses, over the years and decades. The big predators smooth the curves that otherwise would be so ragged from natural variation in the environment that few people would be able to tell what's going on. And when the big predator is doing OK, people are happy. They love the spice that the predator brings into their world. They like that little bit of fear invoked by real or imagined danger. And some are inclined to seek it out. I'm so inclined and so are many of my associates, colleagues, and friends.

I fish and hunt and prowl and ramble where there are big things that can bite. I've been around a lot of lions in East Africa and have pitched my tent in places where they roared all night. I've encountered leopards in the jungle of Malaysia while exploring the headwaters of major rivers. I've been chased by grizzly bears in Alaska and I've trapped black bears in Arkansas. I've had successful hunts for bear and wolf, and I've caught lots of sharks. I've pulled seines in southern backwaters and sloughs while large alligators cruised by. As long as the alligators were up on top, I continued with my work. When they submerged, I got out of the water. I have great love and respect for predatory animals of all sorts and for the places where they dwell. But the one predator that bears my mark, the one that has taken me to the greatest adventures, consistently, and with the keenest sense of purpose in our encounters, has been the flathead catfish.

I've interfaced with this fish now for over half a century. I've caught them with nets, traps, set hooks, and my bare hands.

Strangely, however, I've never fished for them with a rod and reel. I've never felt the need to do that. I've also never felt the desire to shoot a bear with a slingshot.

I've caught thousands of flathead catfish, and among them there were hundreds that exceeded forty pounds in weight. They fought me like tigers every single time. Not one of them came to the boat peacefully. I've had as many as five flathead catfish weighing fifty or more pounds each in one hoop net, and me alone trying to pull the net into the boat while the fish were working and fighting together for common cause *inside the net*—going the other way. Yes, I've caught thousands but, to my knowledge, among the thousands I've caught, I've only killed three of them.

I killed that very first one that I caught as a boy and it fed my family. I had one that attacked my boat in the Tallahatchie River in northwestern Mississippi and, when it rammed into the side of my boat, it actually killed itself. I was able to recover that fish. It weighed eighty pounds and is the largest I've ever had my hands on. I do not know why it attacked my boat. I've never heard anybody else tell of experiencing a flathead catfish attacking a boat. Back in my laboratory at Mississippi State University, I aged this fish by counting the rings of a thin section of one of its pectoral spines under a microscope. It was thirteen years old. The third flathead catfish I've killed in my life was a fish that I caught in the spring of 2014 with a friend when I was sixty-three years old. It was a beautiful fish that weighed just a tad less than twenty pounds. I didn't weigh it, however. I like mystery and, as a fisherman, I really don't want actual data. I prefer the guess. The story is worth telling.

My fishing partner was Larry Deeter. Larry and I have been good friends since about the time I caught that first flathead catfish as a boy. We share many common denominators. We went to the same schools in North Little Rock, Arkansas, and were in many of the same math and science classes as high school students. We both spent time in Southeast Asia as young men. We both married lovely and loving Asian women. His wife is Vietnamese. My wife is Chinese Panamanian. We are blessed with the beauty and magic and mystery of Asia every day in our homes . . . homes that understand the importance of fishing and how important it is for people to share time together in a boat.

Larry is an incredible fisherman and fishes both freshwater and saltwater. His boats are well built and superbly engineered specifically for his purposes. He is a brilliant man who has the incredible discipline of an engineer's mind and equally incredible skills with tools and materials. He can design, build, and maintain practically anything that he needs. He has a good heart. He is also a very kind and thoughtful man who enjoys laughing. He is fun to be with. We decided that we'd go fishing together. We also decided that we'd go to one of our old haunts, Lake Ouachita in western Arkansas, and try to catch a flathead catfish.

Lake Ouachita is located deep in the Ouachita Mountains, northwest of Hot Springs, Arkansas. It is the state's largest lake. Most of its shoreline is wild and undeveloped, as are its many islands. There are vast areas of open water, tens of thousands of acres, and countless secluded coves. The shorelines and surrounding mountains are covered by forests of mixed pine and hardwood. The water is clear and of the highest quality. During the warmer months the lake attracts lots of boaters and anglers, particularly on weekends and holidays. But the large size of the lake generally precludes crowding, especially along the north shore.

As young men, Larry and I frequented the waters along the lake's north shore, but we mostly conducted our ventures alone. I canoed and camped and only fished a little. Larry was more focused on fishing, and particularly, fishing for flathead catfish. Our lives drifted but crossed paths again and again over the years. Then, in retirement, we were drawn closer to each other. We had a shared history, but, more importantly, we recognized the potentials of a shared future.

We decided to go to Lake Ouachita during late spring when the catfish were moving up into the shallows. Larry had the perfect boat for running trotlines: a reinforced aluminum flat-bottom boat with a fine two-stroke, fifteen-horsepower outboard motor. And, from his many years of experience running trotlines along the north shore of the lake, he knew the best set places, he knew the best bait, and he knew how and where to get that bait.

Larry is a retired Air National Guard sergeant and, subsequently, had access to the National Guard's facility that's located on the north shore of Lake Ouachita. That retreat would be our camp. When we arrived at the facility, after a challenging drive over some pretty steep hills on very rough roads, we stowed our personal gear and our groceries in one of the cabins and then launched his boat. Armed with worms and light spinning rods we motored across an open chute to a rocky shoreline and fished for bait. We wanted large sunfish, the larger the better. After about an hour of fishing we had what we needed. There were about forty nice sunfish in the boat's live well. With bait secured, we cranked the motor and took off for another, distant part of the lake that Larry thought would be good for our fishing.

The water was clear, and the sky full of light. The light played on the mountains and sparkled on the water. It had been many years since I'd last been on this lake and much longer since I'd been up on the lake's north shore. With the passage of time I'd anticipated a lot of change . . . to the landscape . . . to the water. I thought that

I'd see the typical evolution of development, with lots of vacation homes and cleared forestlands. But that was not the case.

After more than forty years it was still wild and awesomely beautiful. There was quiet and space and a sense of the pristine. It filled my heart with song. There were mountains and islands everywhere. I had to remind myself where I was—only three hundred miles from my home in Mississippi and only about seventy-five miles from my other home in central Arkansas, the home that serves as my refuge and sanctuary, the place I go to for writing and music—and that this was no distant land. This was my backyard. I'd anticipated change over the decades . . . and disappointment. But there was neither. My reunion caused my spirit to soar.

Larry's gift to me was not just a trip focused on catching a fish that we both like very much. His real gift was that of reminding me, perhaps inadvertently, that I am inextricably linked to the land of my youth, that this land along the north shore of Lake Ouachita, and all it is and all that it proclaims, is still in fine shape, and that I belong to it and it to me.

The power of those revelations was almost overwhelming. They generated a deep glow within me. As I looked around me, at the mountains and the water and the islands, at my friend and his fine boat, and contemplated what we were about . . . fishing for flathead catfish, I was perhaps the happiest man in the world.

After crossing an expanse of open water, we cruised among standing dead timber along one of the islands. There was a small point of land projecting out into the lake that gave the place some shelter. But the air and the water were so still that shelter was not needed.

As the evening deepened, we stretched our lines and baited them with the sunfish that we'd caught. The surroundings, the quiet, and the rich conversation worked on my soul. I looked at the sky as the sun moved down toward the tops of distant mountains. I looked down through the clear water, at our lines, at the rocks and plants below. There was hardly a whisper of wind. I could hear a summer tanager in the darkening forest just beyond the shoreline. Within less than an hour, our three lines were set and we began the journey back across the lake to our cabin.

As the boat skimmed along the surface, I realized that we were practically alone out there on the waters. There were only a couple of boats in the distance, and one belonged to another friend of Larry who also was setting lines for the night and who would share our cabin and meals. Aside from those two boats, we were alone on this immense mountain lake.

From time to time Larry would slow the boat and we'd talk about what we saw and what we were experiencing and about the importance of having a place to go like this where we could set lines with the hopes of catching a big flathead catfish. Other species of catfishes were fine to catch and eat, but we wanted flatheads—the tigers, the top fish in the system, the principal predator that lurked and prowled as a creature of the night and that would indiscriminately devour any living thing that would fit into its mouth . . . which, by the way, is an important thing to emphasize.

Unlike other North American catfishes (channel catfish, blue catfish, and the various species of bullhead catfishes), flathead catfish will not eat dead things. Flathead catfish will only eat things that they personally kill. They are predators, not scavengers. And the bigger the prey, the better. They like their meals in big chunks. I can relate to that.

The sun set and dark settled on us before we were able to get back to the cabin. Insects emerged from the water and filled our eyes and mouths. Larry doesn't wear glasses. I do. So after about ten minutes he asked me to drive the boat. He couldn't see well enough to drive because the insects kept on getting into his eyes.

We swapped places in the boat. I took over the tiller and Larry hunkered down beside my dog, Hank, on the other end of the boat. I could see stars overhead and the shadows of the shoreline on either side of me as I drove the boat through the chute back to the cabin. The dock had no light, but it didn't matter. I could see well enough to find it. That was enough.

Once back at the cabin, and joined by Larry's other friend, who also had just returned from setting his trotlines, drinks were poured and steaks were grilled. Potatoes were shoved into a microwave oven, and salad was prepared. It was about as stress-free a situation as three fishermen can have. There were stories shared and more drinks poured. After the dishes were washed I tried to stay awake for more good conversation but faded quickly. Finally, I surrendered, called my dog, and crawled into my sleeping bag on one of the cabin's bunk beds.

I think I rolled over one time and then it was dawn. I heard Larry stir. He turned on the cabin's lights and made a pot of coffee. We'd go check our lines first off, then come back for breakfast. I could feel the excitement swell within me and could sense it also with Larry. Checking trotlines early on a spring morning is somewhat equivalent to being a child on his way to a Christmas tree to open presents on Christmas morning. And when there are hopes for a flathead catfish, they are roughly the same as the child's hopes for a new bicycle, shotgun, or pony.

The air was cool but not crisp as we motored away from the dock and out into the lake. The hooded sweater I wore felt good. As we rounded the second bend of the chute and moved into the open water of the main lake, I saw several boats positioned and quietly waiting for signs of fish surfacing. These were striped-bass anglers who would cast to the big fish when they came up to slash schools of shad. We moved on past these anglers, keeping our distance from them out of respect for their space and their activity.

When we got to our first line, it was stripped bare of bait and held only one fish, a channel catfish that weighed about two pounds. I concluded that the stripped line was the work of turtles or, perhaps, an otter. The second line held five very nice channel catfish in the four- to six-pound range. After removing the fish from those lines, we left them in place. They would be re-baited and fished again later that day.

We then proceeded to our third and final line. It was wedged under a stump and obviously had been subjected to a lot of tugging and twisting. We could not work it free from the end of the line where we'd started, so went to the opposite end and worked from there.

It was then that we could feel the heavy weight of fish on the line. The first fish was a small flathead catfish that weighed about two pounds. The next hook, however, held a *real* flathead, weighing nearly twenty pounds.

It was a lovely fish, golden with dark flecks, its fins in perfect shape, without a bruise or blemish anywhere on its body. It fought the hook, the line, and us very hard. But once we got it into the boat, I held it hard by the tail and it became quiet. Over the years I've learned this secret. Grab a catfish hard around the tail, squeeze top to bottom, and the fish will not move.

This last fish, this beautiful flathead, would go back to camp with us. As the fisheries biologist and poet in our group, I would be, by unspoken consent, the person to kill and process it—the third flathead catfish I'd ever killed in my life. There had to be efficiency, framework, spirit, and reverence melded into one element in this process . . . call it prayer if you will, or perhaps sacrament. Regardless, the currents were very, very deep.

I felt no sadness in the killing this fish . . . nor do I feel any remorse. It was the proper thing to do. The fish, once killed and processed, was shared among us, strengthening the bridges that linked us to each other and also linked us to place, time, and purpose.

This fish also was shared with another old friend who was unable to join us physically on this trip, but who had been with us in spirit as we'd crossed the bridges on that venture. There was magic in our reunion as we dined in my sanctuary. New bridges were built and old ones strengthened as fine wine was poured and flathead catfish fillets were served. As the hour and the conversation deepened, as we crossed the bridges again and again, I reflected on the ways that flathead catfish have touch my life and the lives my friends.

Flathead catfish, the tigers of the murky depths, have built an incredible number of bridges that proclaim universal synergism among outdoorsmen and others with a sense of environmental stewardship. The bridges that flathead catfish built during my early life helped me to understand who I was as a person—as a creature in a created world—and how big predators fit into the scheme of things. Flathead catfish were critical developmental elements in the bridges of evolving awareness and understanding during my formative years, as I learned how to live with rivers and how to be a naturalist and scientist. These bridges launched me into and sustained a career in fisheries and river conservation in North American and around the world. During this pilgrimage, the tiger's bridges provided me with an essential operational framework as I plunged into new, varied, and incredibly challenging public and political arenas, arenas where a focus on this tiger was the magic key, a common denominator, a treasured and respected reference point, and a gateway to understanding about rivers, our connections with them, and our responsibilities toward them. But beyond all of this, it is this tiger, and the bridges it has built, that consistently linked me to people and places that I love. I suspect it will continue to be this way beyond sunset. I hope so anyway.

Stikine Cabin

...

DUCK HUNTERS HAVE THE PRIVILEGE OF ENGAGING SOME OF the world's most vibrant places under some of the most extreme conditions. We slog and muck and beat our way through frozen, ice-bound, flooded forests, across seemingly endless marshes and muddy fields that stretch to the horizon and beyond, throwing ourselves with reckless abandon into watery, muddy wilderness of every stripe, places that are literally crawling with all sorts of biting things (think alligator, cottonmouth, clouds of inch-long mosquitoes, black flies, brown bears). We stumble and slash our way along ditch banks choked with blackberry brambles and blaze impossible trails through swamps laced with vines that make Jack's beanstalk appear to be a potted plant. We venture out before dawn in tiny boats, with the wind going berserk, plowing our way across dark and frigid rivers and lakes that are ready and more than happy to suck us down into a watery grave. We travel great distances and spend a lot of money to be sweat drenched, near heat stroke, cold, wet, muddy, exhausted, and hungry in lonely lands where the sun bakes us, lightning tries to fry us, winds try to blow us away, icy rains take us to the edges of hypothermia, sleet stings the face, tides trap us, and we know that a slip in the muck or a wave over the bow could mean that our spouses will suddenly become incredibly rich. If we are lucky, we have friends to share the misery and spouses who just shake their heads at our insanity.

With this as the operational framework, the question that bubbles to the top of thought among rational people is "Why?" But duck hunters are not necessarily rational people. They are obsessed people. They are fixated on the beauty of sunrises, the grace of pintails, the magic of mallards cupped over decoys, the brilliance of flooded, frozen woodlands, the magnificence of wilderness, the sweetness of lonely land, the rush of teal, the squeal of wood ducks as they twist through the trees, the symphony of geese, the high, sweet call of trumpeters, the bond between man and dog, the bond of man to man, the bond of man to earth and universe.

Duck hunters will risk all to be there. They abandon (albeit temporarily) family, home, work, community, and anything else in the "other" world that, for whatever reason, is apart from the world where stiff wings whisper. It is not that duck hunters don't care. It is that they tend to care too much. They know the depths of the human soul in ways that others cannot comprehend. For, you see, waterfowl hunting is a religion. Shotguns, boots, dogs, hip boots, waders, and boats are sacraments that reveal elements of truth. The smell of burnt gunpowder is our incense. Incantations flow heavenward from finely tuned calls . . . and are answered by the heavenly hosts that circle our decoys on clear and brittle mornings.

I am in this tribe. I will go, day after day, even if there are few ducks flying, just to be there. And when the ducks are there, the deepest currents of the human oversoul flood my heart. I cannot imagine not going. I cannot imagine not being there. And so, when my friends Mark Stopha and Alan Burkholder asked me to come hunt the Stikine River's tidal flats in Southeast Alaska, there could be only one answer: "When do you want me there?"

I'd known both men for a very long time. Alan had been a graduate student at the University of Alaska in Fairbanks back when I was a young, black-bearded, assistant professor on the faculty there. He'd taken a couple of fisheries classes that I'd taught. We quickly connected as friends, transcending the realms of academia. One day, on a bus that served as a shuttle from the upper to the lower campus at the University of Alaska, I'd met Mark. He was the bus driver. We talked about the Peace Corps (I'd been a volunteer in Malaysia). He said, "That's for me!" and joined up.

After a few years in West Africa and a couple back in Alaska to let the dust settle, he'd come to Mississippi State University to work with me on a river fisheries project. In short order Mark knocked out his master's degree in fisheries and went back to Alaska. Both men now were biologists with the Alaska Department of Fish and Game.

✦ ✦ ✦

It was mid-October when I flew to Juneau to link up with Mark. We then flew together down to Ketchikan to meet Alan. He and Alan had made arrangements with a friend there to transport us by boat out to a US Forest Service cabin on the Stikine River flats. We had lunch at a local café, then went to the harbor to meet their friend and load the boat.

The trip out to the Stikine River flats was gorgeous. The hills were covered by forest that seemed to rush down to the ocean. The water was magic, changing colors as light sifted down through openings in the clouds, transitioning from deepest blue to pastel green and, as we approached the Stikine River, the slightest tinge of gray. Eagles and gulls soared over us. We could see surf smashing into rocky beaches and enchanted coves that oozed mystery. From time to time we spotted seals.

We made our way across some open water with waves just large enough to occasionally send a bit a spray over us. Then, very carefully, we drove the boat up through channels that coursed through the Stikine delta tidal flats. Finally, in the distance, dancing in and out of fog and mist, we could see our cabin. It stood there above all the surrounding area, like a castle on a hill, a rugged structure built on top of two huge spruce logs naturally anchored, embedded actually, on a parcel of tidal flat somewhat higher in elevation than the rest of the area.

The tide was high but slack when we came in, so we were able to bring the boat right up to the cabin's rough wooden porch. Time was of the essence. We had to be fast because once the tide began to fall it would do so very quickly. The boat's owner, also a duck hunter, had some family responsibilities that evening back in Ketchikan. Getting stranded overnight on the tidal flats wouldn't gain him much mileage on the home front. However, he didn't seem to be in much of a rush. If he were trapped on the flats overnight he'd have to wait until the next tide came. He'd have no choice but to hunt with us the next morning. Much to his disappointment, we quickly unloaded the boat and he was on his way. As we watched him work his way back out through the channels we were surrounded by another tide . . . a tide of awesome solitude.

Inside the cabin there was a stove, a few bunk beds, and an ancient oil lamp. There was a damp mustiness that hung heavy in the cabin's interior, the result of perpetual drizzle and mist that defines Southeast Alaska. The smell of sea and forest and salty mud oozed from the walls, the floor, the beds—everything. There was a much-worn journal on the table. In it were short notes from those who had previously called the tidal flats their spiritual home and the cabin their sanctuary and refuge. The journal was leather bound and covered with mold. It had a greasy feeling in a magnificent sort of way, as one would expect from an ancient text that contained sacred writing. Moss on the outside of the cabin encroached wherever shadow-laced sunlight struck wood.

The cabin was a castle well suited for denizens of middle earth: elves, fairies, hobbits, and other folk in tune and in synchrony with songs that seemingly so few can hear. Duck hunters also hear those songs. I could hear them very clearly in that cabin, that castle, that moss-draped cathedral. They were the songs of whispering wings, living water, and lonely lands echoing across the tidal flats and across the eons of time.

After taking my gear inside to get it out of the drizzly rain, I went back out onto the cabin's deck. I stood there quietly, just look-ing . . . just feeling. I was surrounded by, *engulfed* by, a starkly wild and beautiful place. There were misty mountains in the distance behind us, but in front an almost endless expanse of tidal flats, draped by shimmering curtains of drizzle and fog. I could not see to the edge of the flats.

It was rugged terrain, laced with a network of meandering chan-nels that seemed to lead to nowhere. Scattered about were isolated ponds that captured water during high tides and held it during low tides. Here and there were clumps of drift logs and other woody debris.

People get lost in these flats or trapped or sucked down by bottomless mud, just disappearing . . . never to be found. The tide washes over the hapless ones and eternity continues on its journey. This is wilderness primeval. It's here and you can be in it. But you're on your own buster. You can live here like no other place on earth. And you can easily, very easily, die here.

A wilderness-spawned wind rushed over the flats and tugged at my heart. I felt a surge of energy course through me. I'd felt this energy so many times in Alaska, that razor-sharp edge of being that separates realms of mortality from spirit. I felt it and I loved it. It was as if I were in dreamtime . . . but it was no dream. It was very, very real. Everywhere I looked there were ducks swirling. I could hear geese and swans. The tide was now rushing out. I was, again, exactly where I belonged.

The tides are pretty extreme in this place. At low tide it is possible to walk virtually everywhere. Hip boots or waders are, however, essential. High tide can quickly sneak up on you, particularly if the shooting is good—which it generally is during that time of the year. So, we had to be careful. In fact, we planned our hunts so that we'd scatter across the landscape as soon as low tide made it possible to cross the channel in front of the cabin, and then as high tide began, we'd start back to the cabin. This rhythm defined the extent that we could venture out into the flats. To do otherwise, to forget about the tides, to cross one too many channels, to try to squeeze just one more flock of ducks into the decoy spread, fully aware that the tide was rising, was to court disaster. A few minutes made all the difference.

Distant ramblings are not necessary if one's primary purpose on the Stikine's tidal flats is shooting ducks. The ducks, frankly, didn't consider the cabin as anything threatening. So when the tide was high, we could hunt right beside the cabin or even shoot from the porch! But our purposes transcended the shooting. Our ramblings addressed the aesthetic and the restless ways of duck hunters, who—like the ducks they hunt—cannot stay still. Duck hunters have little choice but to respond obediently to the call of some siren adrift on the winds, the arrangement of stars . . . perhaps, the gravitational pull of the earth. Duck hunting is, above all things, about restlessness and how to deal with it.

That first afternoon there were ducks swarming all over the tidal flats. There is no other way to say it. The ducks were not flying. They were swarming. They enveloped the entire place with flocks so huge they appeared to be clouds. We could stand on the cabin's deck and at any given moment see tens of thousands of ducks. There were also geese scattered here, there, and yon. The migration was on, and we were in the middle of it all. God, it was a lovely thing!

Teal would spin and roar like tiny jets around our cabin. Mallards, pintails, and widgeons swirled and cupped and landed everywhere. Some swam around us, right up to the cabin. Others pitched into the nearby patches of grass, now flooded by the high tide. The sun broke through right at sunset, setting the world ablaze with a golden light, creating a world of the dreamtime full of whistling wings and calls.

We felt absolutely no sense of urgency. The ducks were here. We were here. It was inevitable that our destinies would merge. We would try to conduct ourselves as good Presbyterians, with dignity and good order. But the reality of our connection with what was going on all around us out there on the Stikine flats was that we'd be more like holy-roller southern evangelicals at a summer camp meeting gone wild. A Scottish reserve just didn't fit. The emotion in us was simply too high.

Alan was first in line as chef. He fired up the stove and got things going. First order of business: good, hot, strong coffee. Then he brought out some caribou meat and made a stir-fry with onions and a few peppers, to which he added some spices. Once done, he added a little water to make a gravy. Then biscuits were popped into the oven. Once the biscuits were done, the stir-fry dish with thick gravy was ladled out on top of the biscuits. Coffee was poured, and dinner announced. We came to the rough-hewed table, pulled up equally rough chairs, and gave thanks to God for the blessings known only to duck hunters ... including good food.

After supper we sat on the deck and watched as ducks flooded the tidal flats. The tide was falling rapidly. The ducks were working the edges of newly exposed mud. Water lapped gently against the porch. More and more ducks started pouring into the flats from every direction.

In Alaska I've always been lured by the stillness. But there was nothing still about what we were witnessing. We were engulfed by a constant rush of wings against a background of never-ending quacks and honks and whistles. As the sun set there was a crescendo. The action only intensified. And during the night it never stopped. All night long, as we pulled our sleeping bags close around us, the symphony of waterfowl in full migration continued. Sweeter music has never graced Earth.

At sunrise the tide was again high. We waited until it began to fall then, each of us with a sack of decoys, headed out to find spots to hunt. It was then that I discovered the primary challenge of hunting ducks on the flats.

The ducks were all around us and there were small pockets of water scattered everywhere. The ducks wanted to be in every one of those pockets. But finding a place to hide, within shooting distance of a pocket, was tough. Finally, about four hundred yards from the cabin, I spotted a huge driftwood log with a few other logs and branches wedged into it. It was about thirty-five yards away from a good spot where I could put out a few decoys. It wasn't the best setup, but it was the best that I could find. There just was no other cover—no other place to hide.

Once I had the decoys set, I went back to my "blind" to wait. It didn't take long before ducks began to work my spread of decoys. Most were widgeon and pintails. Occasionally, there were mallards. They came and landed, and I just waited. I wasn't in any sort of hurry at all. More than anything, I just wanted to watch and feel and think about things for a little while.

I could smell the ocean. There was a saltiness to the air. I could smell the mountains and the rivers and the wonderful land beyond the flats. A fine mist settled over the landscape. In the distance a flock of tundra swans worked their way south, their high-pitched calls drifting to me on the still air. I breathed deeply. I was "home." Alaska was all around me, the most wonderful land in the world. Everything is in Alaska—space most of all. I've lived there. Although I always leave, I will always be "Alaskan." And I always come back. In my heart I've never really left.

After perhaps thirty minutes, I loaded my shotgun and became the hunter. The shooting was magnificent that morning. The ducks came well to the decoys. They came in little flocks or pairs or, rarely, a single. They would spot my decoys, make a circle or two, and then come right in.

These ducks were wilderness ducks. They'd had no experience with hunters—knew nothing about decoys or shotguns. I probably could have positioned myself right out in the open near the tidal pools and still have had shooting. When the ducks saw my decoys, all I had to do is quack a time or two on my call to make them commit to coming in. They'd cup their wings and float right into where I was waiting for them.

In Alaska, during the hunting season, ducks don't have the winter plumage that defines them later as they move south on their migrations. Because of this, Alaska has different rules for taking ducks. Alaska doesn't require that hunters identify ducks before shooting. The limit during our hunt was six ducks per day per hunter, regardless of species. That makes perfect sense in Alaska.

Although I did not shoot particularly well that first morning, I collected my six ducks in pretty short order and started back for the cabin. When I got to the channel in front of the cabin I noticed that the tide was starting to come it. The channel was beginning to fill. It had been less than knee deep when I'd left the cabin that morning. Now it was nearly to the top of my hip boots and rapidly increasing in depth. There was also a wind coming off the mountains and sweeping across the flats toward the sea. Mark and Alan were still out on the flats. But they are experienced Alaskans. They would know to go to higher ground if necessary. I didn't worry.

I decided that it would be good to start cooking up a lunch. When Mark and Alan got back to the cabin, they would be past ready for it. I crossed the channel, climbed up onto the porch, and went inside. Once inside, I stoked the fire in the wood stove and put on a pot of coffee. Then I rummaged around in our food stores, found a sack of potatoes, a few cans of concentrated milk, and some smoked salmon. Hot chowder would be the perfect thing to knock the chill from duck hunters. I could hear the wind getting stronger. Then, faintly, I also heard the calls of sandhill cranes. I looked outside and saw four cranes in the distance, fighting the wind, coming my way. They didn't seem to be making much progress, but their course, if kept, would bring them right over the cabin. I put two heavy goose loads in my shotgun and set it beside the cabin's door.

I turned again to the task of preparing lunch, occasionally glancing out the cabin door to see what progress those cranes were making. I diced the potatoes into small chunks to help speed the cooking, mixed the condensed milk half and half with water, cut the salmon into spoon-sized pieces, added a half of an onion, and set the mix on the stove. The cranes called again, loudly. I looked and they were about a hundred yards from the cabin's porch, still fighting the wind, still on course. After quickly checking the chowder to be sure it wouldn't boil over, I went to the door, grabbed my shotgun, pumped a shell into the chamber, and waited in the shadows.

The cranes kept coming, sixty yards . . . fifty yards . . . forty yards. I waited until they were almost on top of the cabin and stepped out. I swung on the first crane and shot. It crumpled and fell straight down toward me. I had to jump out of the way as it hit the porch's deck beside me. I pumped the gun again and held on another crane, shot, and saw it fold and hit the water beside the cabin. The only thing that could have made that shooting any better would have been for the cranes to have caught fire as they fell. I was ecstatic!

The crane on the porch deck wasn't going anywhere. But the one in the water was drifting with the incoming tide. So I scrambled over to the canoe we'd brought with us, launched it from the porch, and paddled out to retrieve the bird. These were the first cranes I'd ever shot. They were huge. They were beautiful. And I knew also that they are considered the finest game bird there is on a dinner plate—the beefsteak of the waterfowler's cuisine.

Just as I was picking up my second crane I heard a call. I turned and saw Mark and Alan, stranded on the other side of the channel with Alan's dog, Elvis. The channel was now too deep for them to cross. The wind was blowing much stronger and the incoming tide was starting to get a chop to it.

In the ten minutes or so since I'd launched the canoe, the wind had increased to the point that the bow now became a sail. About all I could do was steer the thing. Mark and Alan saw what was happening and set up the runway for me. I steered the canoe between the two men and they caught it as I rushed by. By the time

I got to where Mark and Alan were standing at the edge of the channel, the water was high on their waders. The channel itself was now over their heads. I didn't have much time to get them across.

Both are big men. Big men in chest waders need to be careful when getting into a canoe, and particularly so when entering from deep water. Alan said Mark needed to cross first and helped him get into the canoe. I took Mark across, held the canoe steady as he climbed onto the porch, and returned for Alan. The tide was already at the top of his waist by the time I got to him. Elvis was swimming around him.

I don't know how he did it, but as I watched, Alan launched himself, rolled into the canoe, and just crouched there, unmoving. It was an amazing feat. Alaska is full of them.

I paddled Alan across. Elvis swam alongside the canoe. Mark crouched on the porch, ready to steady the canoe and help Elvis climb out of the water. Alan first put his gun on the porch and then their ducks and my crane. He and Mark had done very well. Alan had also gotten a "cackler," a small strain of Canada goose. Then, one at a time, Alan and I crawled up onto the porch. Mark grabbed Elvis by his collar and pulled him onto the porch. We then hauled the canoe out of the water and secured it along the side of the cabin.

The wind began to howl. The crests of larger waves washed across the porch. We were suddenly surrounded by a rolling brown sea covered by whitecaps. We stood there for a few minutes watching the incredible wildness of a day suddenly transformed by tide and wind from serene, open tidal flats, with hardly a breath of wind stirring, into a powerful, raging ocean full of fury. Then the wind increased from howling into tempest. It was incredible . . . and it was beautiful to the extreme.

Ducks were now desperate, wheeling everywhere in ragged flocks, looking for safe harbor. The lee side of the cabin provided just enough protection from the wind to make it what the ducks were looking for. There was no other cover. And so, as we watched, flock after flock of ducks pitched into that tiny little refuge from the wind. They could see the cabin from afar, the only landmark on the flats, and they set their course accordingly.

We had our ducks for the day and so only watched the magic. And even had we wanted to shoot, it would have been unthinkable under those conditions. Shot ducks would be lost. There was no way to launch or handle the canoe to retrieve them. The wind and waves were too extreme. And to use a dog was out of the question. The dog would go, but would become lost in the valleys of rolling seas.

After watching for a few minutes, we turned and went inside the cabin, to the coffee and the fire. Boots and coats were hung to dry (a relative term in Southeast Alaska), and guns were wiped, cleaned, and oiled. The woodstove knocked the chill from the air, and just a little of the dampness. We padded around in short boots and slippers, adjusting gear and beds, sorting supplies, "piddling" as only hunters in camp can piddle. We took stock of our supply of dry wood and realized that we'd need to go foraging the next day. Even at high tide, there would be portions of driftwood above the water level that would be dry enough to get fires going. And once we had a fire going, we could get wet wood to burn ... eventually.

And so we established our cozy hunters' camp in the cabin. Each man with his own private space, as on a ship, the essential sacred space from which we'd drift back from time to time into community and comradeship around the fire in the woodstove and the table. There is dignity and unspoken grace in such a hunter's camp. Good food, strong coffee (always going, always hot), and rich conversation turn such a camp into one of the most treasured of all human habitations. It has been this way since the beginnings of humankind.

I think that it is fire, however, that ultimately brings grace to the hunter's camp. It is fire, above all else, that separates us from the other denizens on earth. The ability to create it, tend it, and manage it has been our greatest accomplishment through the tumbling generations, across the eons of time. Look into the fire of a hunter's camp, feel its warmth, and it is impossible not to become a spiritual being. Capture its glow and you capture your humanity. Eternal secrets dance within the flames.

The day faded but the wind continued to howl. We moved closer to the fire and to each other. The chowder took a little longer to cook than originally planned, but that was of no matter. We opened bags of bread and made sandwiches of assorted lunchmeat and spicy mustard. The longer the chowder simmered on the top of that stove, the richer it became, filling the cabin with its aroma, one in sensual synchrony with our wilderness surroundings.

We plucked and cleaned our birds and placed them on a shelf to cool and mellow. We turned up the oil lamp, creating a world of shadows inside the cabin. Eighteen ducks, a goose, and two cranes take time to clean, if done correctly. But by the time we finished, lunch was a fading memory, it was dark outside, and the chowder was ready, thick and creamy and hot. There was over a gallon of it, and an hour later it was all finished.

I volunteered to be the "camp man" the next day, to stay around the cabin, preparing meals, organizing things, drifting occasionally out to the porch, drifting occasionally into the dreamtime, into the land of the never-never. I would cook ducks and perhaps do some baking and—in the magic of all that camp cooking entails—allow the essence of our hunters' camp, the cabin, the wind, water, and waterfowl that surrounded me to continue charging the batteries of my soul. I might venture out just a little . . . if the mood struck me. But I wouldn't go far. The journey I had in mind was of a different sort.

After we cleaned our cooking gear, the light was dimmed and we each retreated to our bunks. We read by flashlight (always take books on an Alaskan hunting trip). I also wrote in my journal. I could hear the lapping of waves against the spruce logs that held our cabin. I could hear the wind, undiminished but, with the falling tide, unable to keep the rolling sea alive. And I could hear the symphony of restless waterfowl. Alan turned off the lamp. There was quiet among us, with only the rustle of pages turning beneath tiny spotlights and the scratching of pen on paper in my journal.

And, at the end of this, the first day of our hunt on the Stikine tidal flats, I reflected on this wild and wonderful and wet and windy world that surrounded me—my world, the world of a duck hunter—and whispered to myself, "It is good."

Mark heard my whisper, and I heard him say, ever so softly, "Yes."

Across Boundaries of Scale

...

THE BOAT SHUTTERED AS IT SLAMMED INTO THE SEAS THAT were building at the end of Southwest Pass, one of the South Louisiana distributaries of the Mississippi River, leading into the Gulf of Mexico. The waves came from two directions simultaneously, primarily from the southwest but also from the west. Those from the southwest were pure and formed directly from wind. Those from the west were echo waves reflecting back at us from a shallow bar that reached out into the ocean. Together, they made a horrendous chop that took our boat to its limits. The boat was simply too small for the world that surrounded us. We had crossed a critical line.

The boat's engine fought with all its might to climb the ten-foot-high waves, and then, while on the crest, and before slipping down into deep and churning valleys, we were tossed about by the chop, a chop that added another three feet or more to the primary wave height. It was not simply dangerous. It was life threatening. But there was no way to turn back around that didn't result in a broadside hit from the walls of water. Then the fury increased. It engulfed us. We realized that we had no choice. We had to try. We had to retreat, turn back—or die.

Somehow we were able to do it. We were able to take advantage of one of the larger waves that had a somewhat less acutely angled slope, and when on it we slid around into position. We were able to ride that monster wave, and then others that came after it, back to the mouth of the pass, and back into a world where we fit somewhat better.

As we entered the relative safety of North America's largest river, there was silence onboard. There were moments of quiet reflection, moments of thanksgiving, moments of prayer . . . and then a little nervous chatter among us. It had been a close call. The ocean, once again, had reminded me of the lesson it has been trying to teach me for a very long time. And somehow, again, in the process, I'd survived. Perhaps someday I'll remember that lesson, the lesson about resolution and its sister, scale. Perhaps . . .

Ah, yes, *resolution.* The ability to discern. The capacity to cope. The juxtaposition of self in time and space. And *scale*, a sense of place. A sense of position, of being, that transcends the immediate and evolves ultimately into universal dimensions. A copepod in my fishless woodland pond lives out its entire life much the same as does a whale in the ocean. It's all a matter of relativity. In relative terms, both dwell in a boundless expanse, and yet neither will encounter the other. Resolution probably matters to them, but scale probably doesn't.

It seems that scale really matters only to critters, like certain types of human beings, who tend to thrive on regularly crossing spatial and temporal boundaries. Poet-naturalists with a smidgen of science in their operational framework qualify on all counts. Add to this a propensity for adventure and a poorly camouflaged lust for the sting of battle, and all hope for a quiet and orderly life is thrown as dust (or perhaps sea spray) to the four winds.

Members of this tribe, my tribe, are the restless ones of the species, forever dealing with the concept of scale and, in the process of doing so, perpetually finding it necessary to engage in transcendence. We are forced to cut across those boundaries, to engage new realities regarding fit. We are trying to find a place in the scheme of things—if we can—trying to make sure that senses are tuned in on the proper resolution channel for that realm of being.

We tend to kid ourselves, playing games with the mind as we listen to our hearts and souls. We think we fit, when in reality we don't. We move boldly forward and then find ourselves eyeball to eyeball with the unexpected. It can take our mortality to a very keen edge. The slightest misstep can spell the end. But we do it anyway. We go. We do. We have no choice but to try.

Fortunately for the likes of us, the restless ones, there is the sea. We can ignore the sea, for a while perhaps, but eventually it wins. Its call is relentless—and, for me, terrifying. I go to sea regardless of my fears. I am drawn to the sea because it explodes the boundaries of scale. Life began there and, as I am all too well aware, it can end there. For me, it probably will.

I've gone to sea in huge ships, year after year, through an entire career in fisheries, working weeks at a time on the decks of matchsticks tossed in tempests, melding my rhythms with those of the ship and the sea and the sky and learning every time, always, that nothing in that mix ever stays the same. Every time I go to sea I realize once again that a ship is only big when in port. The sea overwhelms whatever we call "big."

I've sailed many seas in small boats, sometimes powered by wind, sometimes by engine. I've sailed under the Southern Cross in the tropics and under the Great Bear off the coast of Alaska. I've navigated around coral reefs and icebergs. I've gone beyond the relative safety of coastal estuaries, lagoons, and bays and entered open oceans—the Atlantic, the Pacific, the Indian—in a tiny skiff and just kept going as the swells gathered strength and my little boat climbed their peaks. I've been caught in doldrums and ground by surf upon coral. I've been smashed against rocks and sucked into storms above and below the equator. I've been entranced by sunlight penetrating waves off the stern and within those waves that towered above me, recognizing my insignificance as I looked through the waters and saw huge sharks that were trailing my boat . . . just waiting. The water, the light, the sharks were at once beautiful and terrifying. I've watched the magic of phosphorescent light streaming behind my boat's rudder as I steered by the Southern Cross. I raced before waterspouts. I've clapped with delight at porpoises leaping in bow waves of my boats and cursed marauding sea lions that stripped salmon off my lines before I could get the fish into the boat. I cannot turn the sea loose. And the sea will not turn me loose.

In almost all ventures out to sea I was chasing fish. That was my license, my passport, my ticket to enter the realm. But it has never been about the fish. They served mostly as sacraments, bridges to something beyond the present but inextricably linked to it. They were, however, strange bridges because there was never a foundation to anchor them—only a "spaceship," a life-support system, bobbing about on the space of the ocean's surface. Yet without those tiny floating cocoons it would have been impossible to be there. Thus, the boats.

I live and am alive *because* of boats. My life was forged in them. My career was conducted in them. And only because of them have I been able to transcend the many different boundaries of scale that the sea can create. I have never been in love with boats, but we've always gotten along well together. They have been marriages of convenience.

As is the case with other types of marriages, some boats are beautiful and some are purely functional. When you have both in one package, it can be wonderful. On that day in Southwest Pass, as my long-time friend Larry Deeter, his son Paul, and I were trying to make our way out through the waves into the Gulf of Mexico and found that such passage was impossible, we were blessed by being in a boat that qualified as "wonderful" in every sense of the word.

It was a good boat, a "C-Dory," twenty-two feet long, superbly engineered, with high bow, flat bottom, and plenty of room. There was a cabin forward and an open fishing deck aft. It was equipped with good electronics for navigation out into a world beyond our evolutionary echoes. It was not a fast boat, but it was strong. Had that not been the case, and had Larry not been the exceptional skipper that he is, I would not be telling this tale. I had faith that day in the boat and in the skipper. My faith in the boat, however, was first and foremost founded upon my faith in the skipper.

But the sea can throw unexpected forces at you. And when it did on that day, three men and a boat discovered a new boundary. That was and remains a good thing. We were not able to fish as planned that day, but we came back with something even more important, and not just our lives. We had, rather, *lived*—danced on the edge, flirted with powerful elements that forced us into the precious dimensions of the present tense, which, after all, is all we ever really have anyway. And that is why I will keep going back to the terrifying sea.

But it is not always terrifying, at least not on the surface of things. It is easy to forget, to push aside the terror, to pretend that the monster is just an illusion. And so, the previous day, the day before the waves at Southwest Pass, we had fished in the glory of light, sparkle, and beautiful water. The ocean was resting that day, gently moving, calling to us, inviting us to skim along its surface and probe its depths, beyond sight of land and into the realm of great fish.

For more than an hour, beyond the end of the river, we traveled out to sea. We were well equipped and well provisioned. The magic surrounded us. We fell into the mariner's trance, sensing the deep rhythms of nature. Birds wheeled around us. Small fish swirled occasionally on the surface. When we needed bait, Paul would cast out with a light, spinning rig that had several small jigs tied to it. Rarely was there a cast without hits. Frequently, every hook would hold a fish. These baitfish, called "hardtails," would weigh up to a pound apiece. The bigger the bait, theoretically, the bigger the fish that we'd likely hook.

I cannot argue about that theory because we caught lots of very large fish. We caught and released sharks mostly, and some extremely big red snappers. The sharks averaged around forty pounds each, and the snappers averaged around twenty-five pounds. All were powerful fish that arched our thick-butted, stiff, deep-sea rods. The rods had all the grace of broom sticks—short and virtually impossible to bend by hand. But the fish bent them, and the rods worked their magic, never failing, constantly keeping tension on the fish, wearing them down as the fish wore us down. The fish ripped lines off of our reels, causing the drags to scream. They plunged again and again back into the dark depths of the sea. As we fought those fish, they jerked us all over the back of our boat. Every fish caught was an endurance test. Most were hooked in very deep water, near the bottom. Sometimes the water would be nearly two hundred feet deep. It takes an incredibly long time to get a big fish into the boat when that fish was hooked two hundred feet below the boat. Fortunately, we had enough cold beer onboard to revive us after the fights.

Once we had sharks on the surface alongside the boat, we cut the line to release them. We didn't want snapping jaws and lashing tails onboard. For the snappers, we had a weight tied to a small hook and light line. We'd unhook the larger hook that had caught the fish and attach the smaller hook to the fish's mouth. Then we'd send the fish back down into the depths to relieve the air pressure in its swim bladder. When we jerked hard on the light line, the light line would break, releasing the fish back into the world where it belonged. We did what we could to ensure survival of all but one fish that we caught. The exception was the result of my very last cast of the day.

I hooked a two-pound hardtail on my line as bait and cast it over the side of the boat. In spite of the weight I had on the line (about one pound of lead), the hardtail stayed pretty much on the surface, struggling. That struggling attracted a forty-pound king mackerel. It slashed the bait and immediately was hooked. My rod arched. The reel's drag sang to me. It was all I could do to turn the fish as it bore down as hard as it could, trying to reach an oil rig, where it could break off. Then it began to tire and, after a few more minutes of fighting, I was able to bring it up to the boat, close enough so that Paul could gaff it and bring it onboard. It was an exceptional king mackerel, almost too long to fit into the boat's ice chest. Only by bending the fish double could we get it into the ice chest, and still a portion of its tail flapped outside.

After boating that fine king mackerel, we knew that it was time for the sailors to return from the sea. Standing there on the boat's deck, sun-baked and drenched with sweat, the three of us paused, looked around at the sea, breathed deeply of the salt air and, each in his own private way, acknowledged the power of the sea's song on our hearts. We had absolutely no idea that the next day the sea would test us and test our little boat. Small waves and gentle winds were forecast.

But the sea had other ideas regarding scale. It always does.

Before the Storm

...

THERE WAS A RESTLESSNESS THAT SWIRLED IN THE WINDS OF the November dawn. I tried to ignore it but couldn't. The winds whispered change and adventure. The sky was clear, but there was undeniably something going on. The birds sensed it too. By midday they were flocking and going early to the cutover fields to eat, as they normally would do just before sunset. By 2:00 p.m. I'd given up on trying to do anything constructive at work, locked my office, and headed home. I was pretty sure that deer would be as restless as I was and that they would be moving.

It took me about thirty minutes to shower, dress for the woods, grab my rifle, and start the ten-minute drive down the county road that leads to my farm. After parking my truck at the gate, I noticed clouds building in the west. The wind had stopped swirling and had steadied from the northwest at about five miles per hour.

That was good because, with only one exception, every deer stand on my farm that year could be hunted on a northwest wind. One was in the woods. One overlooked a large hayfield that had a narrow strip of wheat planted along the far edge. One was tucked back into a quiet corner of the farm, overlooking a small clearing that also was planted with wheat.

The pasture would be much too open early in the afternoon, even with the change in weather. It was best suited for still afternoons when the light was fading. It was a twilight stand. The stand in the woods was on a travel corridor, not a destination. It was best suited for frosty mornings during the rut. So I chose the stand back in the quiet corner of my farm. Even though the deer were restless with the changing weather moving in, they'd want to stay tight to cover as they grazed on the young wheat.

By 3:30 I was settled on my stand, enveloped by the magic and the mood of the woods as the clouds thickened. A few minutes later there was a gust of wind. I felt the temperature drop suddenly as it passed. That gust left a little crispness in the air that hadn't been there earlier in the day. Then the wind steadied again. Overhead the clouds grew darker. Although there still were nearly two hours left until sunset, a flock of wood ducks whistled over the treetops and landed in a brushy little pond back in the woods behind me. A Carolina wren that had been probing the leaves on the ground below my stand flitted up to a dead grapevine and disappeared into a small opening where the wood had rotted under the bark. It didn't come back out, so I figured that it was hunkering down for the evening, ahead of the change in weather.

Then I looked up and out across the young wheat in the clearing. When I did so, my heart skipped a beat. There in front of me, grazing on the wheat, was a beautiful eight-point buck. How he'd been able come into that clearing and get out that far into the opening without me seeing him was mystifying. It was as if he'd just materialized out of the earth. Bucks are, however, magic creatures. They do stuff like that. They also can disappear just as quickly, into a vapor apparently of their own creation.

This buck was sleek but very muscular, broad across the back, with well-developed hindquarters and big shoulders. His chest was full and starting to sag just a little. He was a fine three-year-old buck. I knew that I couldn't spend much time admiring him. Bucks like that don't linger long anywhere.

Slowly I raised my rifle and put the crosshairs of the scope on the buck's chest just behind his shoulder. He was quartering toward me just a little, and so I waited. I wanted a clean, broadside shot in order to minimize damage to not much more than a couple of ribs. The rifle was steady. I waited . . .

Then, instead of turning away to give me the shot I wanted, the buck turned and faced me! I held my breath. Although I was in shadow and tucked back into the woods, away from the clearing, I was sure that he would see me. He was less than thirty yards from my stand. He raised his head and looked right at me. I could see him chewing on the wheat he'd just snatched. His ears moved in all directions. He stopped chewing, raised his nose high into the air, and sniffed. I could see his nostrils twitch. I didn't blink. A neck shot was possible. But still I waited, hoping for the broadside shot. I didn't detect tenseness in the buck. He was alert but not tense. Then he lowered his nose and continued chewing on the wheat in his mouth.

A moment later he put his head down to graze more. I kept the crosshairs of the scope on the spot where I wanted to make my shot. The safety was off. My finger was on the trigger. My breathing was slow and steady. He turned back and gave me what I wanted. I touched the trigger. He was knocked over onto his side, kicked twice, and lay still.

Quickly I jacked another bullet into my rifle and kept the rifle pointed at the deer, just in case he recovered from the shock and jumped up. I've had that happen. It is rare, but it can happen. This buck, however, was down.

I unloaded my rifle, climbed down the ladder of my stand, reloaded (just in case), and slowly walked over to the buck, where he lay on the crushed wheat. He was a fine buck with fully formed antlers. I'd thought he was an eight-pointer, but as it turned out he had nine points. For some reason, bucks on my farm typically don't have brow tines, but this fellow had one, a small one on one antler, about two inches long, that I hadn't seen.

Unloading my rifle again and slinging it across my shoulder, I grabbed the buck and started dragging it away from the clearing and toward my pond, about 150 yards away. He was heavy—probably weighing around 180 pounds—large for a Mississippi whitetail. It took some effort to get him moved, but I needed to do it because I don't like to field dress deer on my food plots. Although I'm sure that deer smell me and the blood of deer, I don't want anything other than my scent and a blood trail remaining after a kill.

Huffing and puffing, with both hands full of antlers, it took me about fifteen minutes to get the buck to the edge of the pond. There I stripped down to a T-shirt and quickly field dressed him. Once the task was over, I washed my hands, arms, and knife, put my hunting clothes back on, and looked at the woods and the sky. Hunting conditions were only getting better, in fact, *much* better as the afternoon slipped into evening and the weather front continued rolling in.

The buck would be fine there on the grass beside the pond. I had him propped open so that he'd cool and drain. There really was no reason for me to call it quits for the day . . . and particularly on so special a day. So back I went to the deer stand overlooking the clearing. There was only a small portion of that clearing that had the buck's blood and my scent, and that portion of the clearing was near the stand. Most of the clearing remained "clean" and the wind was still in my favor.

Forty-five minutes after shooting the buck, I was settled again on the stand, watching, feeling, melding with the beauty of the November woods that enveloped me. I heard a rumble of thunder in the distance. A lone wood duck ripped by overhead and splashed into the pond behind me, joining his buddies there. Fifteen minutes later I saw a gray squirrel working its way along an arboreal highway in the topmost branches of some water oaks on the far side of the clearing.

It was starting to get a little dusky. I could still clearly see the other side of the clearing, but back among the trees in the woods it was difficult to make out details. Then, while I was trying to probe those woods with my senses, I thought I saw a slight flicker of movement. I couldn't be sure that I'd seen something. Perhaps it was just my imagination. I keep looking at the spot where I'd seen the movement. It could have been a squirrel or perhaps some bird on the ground. I looked out into the clearing, just to check, then I looked back into the woods. There, near a fallen tree, was a shadow that I didn't remember. I looked harder. The shadow didn't move. I looked back into the clearing, then back to the shadow. The shadow was now moving. It was a deer.

I couldn't shoot the deer where it was. The light wasn't good enough. There was too much chance of hitting an unseen branch or vine and deflecting the bullet. I couldn't be sure of the shot, so I waited. The shadow deer was moving steadily toward the clearing. There was still enough light out there for good shooting. Then, about forty yards away, from behind a big redbud tree that hangs out over the clearing, the deer stepped out into the open.

It was a doe, a big doe, a beautiful doe. It took a few more steps out into the clearing, stopped, and immediately began grazing. The light was quickly fading, but through my rifle's scope I could clearly see the doe. The crosshairs of the scope were sharp and bright. The scope pulled more light into the image. I slipped off the rifle's safety, settled the crosshairs on the doe's chest and touched off the shot. It was the same shot that had put the buck immediately on the ground. But all deer are different.

The doe spun around, made a terrific leap back into the woods from which she'd come, and ran about sixty yards before dropping. I saw where she fell. I could also hear her thrashing in the bushes and leaves on the ground. I could just barely see her, but I knew that she was down.

The run had been the result of a heart shot. I'd shot just low enough to hit the heart. The buck had been shot through both lungs, but I'd not hit his heart. A difference of an inch or two in a chest shot makes a huge difference in the way deer respond to the shot. But regardless, a chest shot is always a killing shot with a proper rifle and the right bullet. I had both that afternoon: a .30-06 Winchester Model 70 rifle with 150-grain soft-nosed bullets. This rifle is a battle-scared old veteran that's taken a lot of deer for me, as well as bigger stuff like bear, elk, moose, wolf, and caribou. I trust the rifle and the load—and that's important.

I unloaded the rifle, climbed down from my stand, reloaded, and started toward the doe. I'd walked perhaps a hundred feet from my stand when suddenly another deer jumped out in front of me, ran twenty feet, and stopped. It was another big doe. I immediately raised my rifle, put the crosshairs of the scope on her, and whispered quietly to myself "bang," mentally dropping her in her tracks. Then I watched as she melted into the deepening shadows of the woods, knowing as I did so that the chances were good that we'd have another encounter before the end of deer hunting season.

I dragged one doe out from the clearing and carried the other one in my heart as I made my way to the pond where my buck lay. When I got there, I couldn't refrain from walking over to the buck, grabbing his antlers, and giving them a little shake. I loved their cool roughness near the bases and the slick and polished tines that finished in wonderfully sharp points. I loved the way he looked, stretched out on the grass by the pond. He was truly a good buck, a magnificent buck, and I was proud of him. And the two does, the one beside the buck as well as the one still slipping through the November woods, were equally magnificent in their sleekness and beauty. All three filled my heart with song.

The weather front arrived just as I finished field dressing the doe beside the pond. The wind picked up and there were big raindrops starting to fall when I got her loaded into the truck. The rain was coming more steadily as I wrestled the buck into the truck's bed alongside the doe. By the time I'd driven back across the pasture to my farm's gate, the rain was falling very hard, the wind had it whipped into a fury, and there was a lot of thunder. Aside from two small spots on the farm, the two places where I'd field dressed the deer, all evidence of the hunt was washed away.

But nothing can wash away the effects of that hunt on my hunter's soul. That was one of the very few times I've shot two deer in one day, and I doubt if there will ever be another. The memories of that hunt before the storm are simply too precious to let there ever be another of its sort. It was the most perfect deer hunt of my life and is etched into the realm of treasured memories . . . to be resurrected on restless days, before future storms, when I may not be able to be out among it all.

Echoes from a Deeper Past

...

THERE ARE CALLS IN THE WILD THAT STIR THE SOUL. STRANGE and yet somehow familiar energy courses through me as wolves fill an Arctic night with song. When I hear wolves I'm forced to leave camp or cabin to wander alone across frozen hills, my way illuminated only by starlight and the shimmering curtains of the northern lights. Although some say it isn't true, I can assure you that you can hear the Aurora crackling as it drips and dances across the heavens. The tonking of nightjars in the Malaysian jungle, the lonesome, eerie, ghost-like call of screech owls in Mississippi on a summer's night, the laughter of hyenas after sunset on the Serengeti, the bass voice of a bullfrog in a Louisiana bayou, the howling of a dingo at dawn in the Australian desert, the bugle of a bull elk in amid Rocky Mountain aspens, the cry of a soaring red-tailed hawk on a still Ozark afternoon, the restless midnight murmuring of gulls on their coastal roosts—all link me to a way, to a state of being, that drifts across the millennia, defining who I am . . . reminding me that, like the other denizens of earth, my genes sing in synchrony with eternal elements. The most powerful, the most stirring, of all wild calls, however, is the call of wild geese.

The call of wild geese, regardless of species, is effused in mystery. It clearly announces and discusses purpose, destiny, and discovery, albeit we know not what they may be. Wild geese know and respond to the rhythms of the earth perhaps better than any living creature and have the propensity to engage in discourse about it among themselves. They are inextricably linked not only to the earth but to one another. They are the champions of fidelity. They are honorable . . . even unto death.

I hunt them. And in doing so, I hunt for myself. When I am among wild geese, I know that I'm in the right place, doing the right thing. Sometimes (rarely), I am able to stalk them, carefully moving as a panther, closing distance through muck and mud and brush, until, finally—revealing myself amid a flurry of beating wings, wild honks, and booms from my old shotgun—there's a melding of almost sacramental destiny. This was, I admit, much easier to do during my twenties than during my sixties.

But most of the time I find out where the geese want to be and try get there before they arrive. When hunting Canada geese, a few decoys can help, if placed correctly, and if the light and wind and the phase of the moon and the alignment of the stars are right. If you're hunting Canada geese, don't worry about scruffy-looking decoys. They have their proper place—in your fireplace. Other geese don't seem quite so picky, most of the time, as long as you've put out a few hundred decoys in a place that the geese have already decided is where they want to go.

Wild geese have a tendency to look over their world, and particularly their landing zone, with the eyes of an imaginative taxonomist. Like the taxonomist, they apparently see things that don't exist, but they *think* they exist and that's all that matters. All it takes is one old goose or gander with a vivid imagination to abort a landing and take the complaining flock to some perceived safer place. Sometimes, when hunting geese, it is best not to do anything at all except hide in the place where you think the geese want to be. Give them nothing at all to look at and they cannot create evil imaginings . . . usually.

Although they sometimes pass overhead, in the stratosphere, snow geese are really not that common in eastern Mississippi. We don't hunt them here. Snow geese are found mostly over in the western part of Mississippi, along the river. Over here in the hill country of eastern Mississippi, where I live, goose hunting focuses on Canada geese. Most of the Canada geese around here are the resident, non-migratory variety, although during late winter we occasionally get flocks of migratory Canadas. The migratory geese seem to be smaller than the resident variety. Regardless, Canada geese are the big game of the waterfowler's world.

I must admit, however, that a hunt that is absolutely focused on Canada geese is sort of rare, except during a special goose season that happens over a two-week period during late summer. Goose hunts are part of a bigger picture, a broader campaign. And, even during these late summer forays, when the goose hunts are focused, they tend to be blended into teal hunts. Set up for teal and you are probably in a good spot for geese. Or perhaps it works the other way. Find the geese first, then go there early in the morning on a teal hunt. If there are teal in the area, they will be there too, usually very early. The geese will come later, after the sun is up. The key to success on these hunts is mostly a matter of remembering to switch loads in your shotgun. The light number four steel shot used for teal tends to make Canada geese laugh at you.

But these hunts can be beyond wonderful . . . way beyond. There's nothing quite so nice as slogging back across flooded marsh and mud flats when the morning sun is a diffused orange ball filtered by the thick, moist air, sloshing and mucking along in waders or hip boots, drenched in sweat, slapping mosquitoes, and hauling a limit of teal, two or three giant Canada geese, a shotgun, and a sack of nondescript duck decoys, kicking cottonmouths out of your way, hollering at your dog to stay close so that he won't get dragged away by an alligator, and trying to blaze a trail up through some overgrown pasture long past due for mowing.

While the rest of the world was yawning, sipping coffee, and heading off to seek their fortunes, you've been out where life is thick and pulsating. And, when you get back to the truck, you celebrate that life—mostly because you were not sure that there would be much more of it in store for you about ten minutes previously.

The birds and the gear are tossed into the back of the truck, the gun is leaned (unloaded) against a front tire (to be run over later), and you reach for your thermos of coffee that is always on the other side of the truck from the door you opened. You shed your waders or boots, strip down to a light cotton shirt, and lean against the truck, coffee in hand. A light breeze dries the sweat on your beaded brow and makes the soaked shirt feel just a little chilly. And then you hear the music, that haunting music of new geese coming to the place that you just left.

You listen and reflect and remember the magic moments earlier that morning when you were there, when you first heard them coming through the hazy dawn. You remember watching a tenseness settle over your dog as he hears the geese and hears you changing loads in the shotgun. And the calls get ever louder, reverberating to the core of your being, and suddenly they are right there, coming in low over the willows, filling the air with their gabble, huge wings pulling at the air, long necks outstretched and pumping in synchrony with the wing beats, dark heads with white cheek patches outlined sharply against the sky, big black feet all splayed, and then the wings cupping as they begin to settle over your duck decoys—and the first shot, and the huge splash as the first goose crashes, and the automatic pumping of the gun, and another shot, and another—and then there before you are three giant birds among the decoys as the other geese beat the air to escape, honking and filling the world with their calls. Two of them are down for the count. One needs a finishing shot. Then and only then do you suck in a deep breath and realize that for the past minute or so you had forgotten to breathe. The dog rushes out and drags the first twenty-pound bird across the mud flat to you, then the next, then the last one. He is doing what he was bred and trained to do, and so are you.

And the new geese are coming in, on those distant mud flats where you were, down below where your truck is parked. You hear them, and you dream of tomorrow, take another sip of coffee, listen some more, realizing that the geese have settled for the day, and call the dog to "load up." Your soul is absolutely stirred. You can't get the call of geese out of your head, nor do you want to.

Later in the season, during winter duck hunts, Canadas prowl the countryside searching for hidden pockets where they will be safe. Quiet, secluded ponds tucked back away from the general world of people and dogs and cattle tend to be their preference. The landscape in eastern Mississippi is full of such ponds, and this makes hunting them for geese completely unpredictable. They may be on a pond today and not come back to it for a week or two or ever.

During the duck season I go hunting almost every morning. And almost every morning I hear Canada geese. When I hear them, my heart skips a beat. Will they come today? I listen, straining to hear, to determine whether or not they are coming closer. Usually the calls fade and I focus back on ducks. But sometimes the geese come.

I quit using Canada goose decoys when duck hunting. They were expensive decoys and I thought they looked just great. But the geese didn't like them at all. The ducks didn't care one way or the other, so I just stopped using them. I found also that the geese didn't like mallard duck decoys. It seems that most duck hunters use mallard decoys and the geese learned all about them. I've had geese coming into my pond over a set of mallard decoys that I'd been shooting ducks over all morning, and the geese would flare and be gone. "No mallards, thank you." Diver decoys were a little better, but the best decoys for Canada geese seemed to be wood duck decoys. Almost nobody that I know uses wood duck decoys. But on my place they make perfect sense because most of the ducks that come to my ponds are wood ducks. Other ducks will also come to wood duck decoys.

When I first got those decoys it was near the end of that year's duck season. I'd been hunting with friends on a place over in Arkansas. After one of our hunts we stopped at a sporting goods store and they had decoys on sale. I saw a box of wood duck decoys and said, "What the heck. I'll give them a try."

When I got back to my Mississippi farm I started using them, and it was like I'd waved a magic wand over my ponds. Ducks that normally would not have dipped a wing at me came into that pond like rockets. All I had were six wood duck decoys, but that's all I needed.

Every day I'd hear geese, but they seemed to hug the tree line way off on the other side of my pasture, heading for who knows where. They showed absolutely no interest in my ponds, and, in fact, I had not taken a single goose during the duck season out there on the place. Then, the very last day of that year's duck season, the geese decided to take a somewhat different route across my farm. Rather than follow the tree line, they flew right up the center of the pasture. The whole farm reverberated with their calls and I was about to go mad and bite myself with anticipation. I could see them clearly. I counted them. There were seventeen of them. They were flying very low, low enough to shoot at, but their route would not, however, bring them across my pond. Then I heard a different sort of call from one of the geese in the flock, and the entire flock wheeled, turned, and started gabbling about landing. Geese get really excited when they make up their minds to land and start making their approach.

There was an ever so slight northwest wind blowing across the pond, directly into the face of the geese. The wind had my wood duck decoys bobbing and darting on top of the pond. The geese didn't hesitate at all. When they got just to the edge of the pond they all cupped their wings and started gliding in for a landing. I waited until two geese were already on the water and then opened up on those still airborne at thirty yards with number two standard steel shot from my old pump gun. The first goose I shot at crumpled and hit the water hard. The rest of the flock starting honking and beating the water and the air, trying to overcome the momentum of landing. They were low and they were close, very close. I was hidden in the shadows of a cedar tree on one of the islands out in the pond. The geese came right by me, no further than fifteen yards from where I was standing. I shot again and down came goose number two. I still had one shell in my shotgun but was so awestruck about what had just happened that I just didn't think about shooting again. A third shot would have completed the three-goose daily limit, but the thought of shooting a third goose never entered my mind. There before me, on the water of my little pond, lay two huge and very dead Canada geese.

My dog, Hank, a wirehaired pointing griffon, waited until I gave him the command to go, then immediately went to the goose that was closest to us. Grabbing it by the neck, he worked hard to get it up to the island to where I could reach out and grab the thing. Hank is a good water dog but somewhat small, at about sixty pounds, for the task of geese. Ducks are his thing. Geese are a challenge.

I put that first goose next to a pair of ducks I'd shot earlier that morning, then sent Hank out for the other goose. It was all the way across the pond on the other side. Hank swam to it and, rather than retrieve it back across the pond, dragged it up on the pond levee and just stood there over it. I shouted for him to bring that goose to me. Hank didn't budge. I shouted again, but still he stayed put. Finally, in exasperation, I crawled out of my hiding spot on the island, sloshed over to the pond bank, and stalked down the levee to my dog and the goose, admonishing Hank for disobedience.

When I got to the goose I reached over and grabbed it by the neck. My gosh, what a gander! Its head was bigger than both of my fists combined. Its neck was as big around as my upper arm. When I held it up, with its beak level with my eyes, its tail was still on the ground. When I stretched its wings out, they were collectively longer than I am tall, nearly six feet. That goose weighed at least twenty-five pounds. I apologized to my dog. He did the only reasonable thing—haul that magnum goose to dry ground and stand guard over it.

Since that special end-of-season hunt with the wood duck decoys, as new seasons have come and gone, joining the ranks of seasons past, Hank and I have shared several fabulous goose hunts together. We've hunted snow geese in flooded rice fields and Canada geese on river sandbars. We've crouched in anticipation as white-fronted geese have worked our mallard and snow goose decoys over in Arkansas. From time to time, the Canada geese have come to my little pond out on my Mississippi farm. Regardless of species or setting, the magnificence and mystery of wild geese, and their haunting calls, never fail to stroke my hunter's spirit, penetrating to its very core.

Through listening, carefully, to the call of wild geese and responding to that call as a hunter, I know better who I am, not only as a hunter, but also as a man. I find myself probing ethereal realms with questions and wonder and hope. The call of geese takes my heart to places I've never been and where I'll probably never go. When the geese come over, full of gabble and heavy wing beats, they bring with them, and share with me, just a little bit of where they've been, where we've all been, through the echoes from a deeper past.

Ferguson's Perspective

...

THE LATE MORNING SUN SENT SHAFTS OF LIGHT STREAMING through the shadows of the October woods. Out in the fields it bathed the land with gold. My friend Sam Gates and I had been walking along a dusty trail for perhaps half an hour, on our way to visit friends and engage in a very special sort of rabbit hunt. We'd left my old Dodge Dart parked at the end of the road, where the trail began. The trail followed the fringes of the lower White River's vast floodplain forest in eastern Arkansas. On that fringe there were fields of soybeans and rice, brown and ready for harvest ... fields broken occasionally by hardwood stands, old sloughs, creeks, and isolated depressions filled with tupelo and cypress. Frost had covered the ground before sunrise, but now, after the sun had knocked the chill from the air, it had all melted. Leaves crunched under our feet as we continued along the trail. Overhead the sky was clear and the deepest of blue—the blue that only comes on autumn days. It was a day perfect for rambling, perfect for meeting up with friends, perfect for a rabbit hunt.

Years before, longer ago than anyone really remembered, somebody had managed to haul an old house trailer back to a pocket of woods near the river and had cleared a few acres around it in a feeble attempt to farm. If there had once been a road to the site, it was now long lost to time and nature's healing processes. Some said that there had never been a road, that the trailer had been brought to the site on a barge or raft during one of the river's great floods, but nobody really knew for sure. Only a few people knew that the trailer even existed, and fewer cared.

The farming venture had languished, and the trailer had been abandoned and left to melt into the ground. But it had not melted. Resting on a foundation of huge cypress logs and situated on the higher ground of a natural levee along one of the unnamed bayous that snaked its way across this part of the river's floodplains, its floor was just high enough that it escaped all but the highest floods.

Its roof was now covered by earth formed from decades of accumulated leaves and wind-blown organic matter of all sorts. From this earthen base the entire roof now was a thick carpet of moss, natural sod that was impermeable. The sides of the trailer were a dull, light green, dusted with gray, a mixture of algae and lichen. There was a covered wooden porch of weathered cypress lumber. The porch was as sturdy as the day it had been built.

As we approached the trailer, a cautious but friendly basset hound barked and ran to meet us. It approached slowly, sniffed us as we stood still at the edge of the small clearing that surrounded the trailer, then wagged its tail and licked our extended hands. A young man came out onto the porch and greeted us. We were expected. He'd invited us to his home the day before during a chance encounter in a state wildlife management area where we had been hunting squirrel. It had been my first encounter with the man, but Sam had apparently had dealings with him before.

The young man was in his late teens, certainly not yet twenty years old. He was tall, lanky, and had a smooth face. He wore old jeans, a plaid shirt, and was in his bare feet. Next to the door of the trailer was a pair of black rubber knee boots. His hair was an oak leaf brown, long and fine textured, reaching beyond the collar of his shirt. He didn't wear a watch. His belt was dark leather, thick and well oiled. The buckle was simple and made of brass. He wore no glasses. His eyes were clear and blue . . . the same blue as that of bluebirds.

There was a gentle rustling behind him. Then, from within the shadows of the trailer came a girl—his wife. She joined him on the porch and smiled at us. She wore a light cotton dress and was beautiful. She had dark, straight hair and facial features that hinted of native blood. But her skin was a lustrous white, smooth and without blemish. Her eyes were darker than her husband's, more gray than blue. She reached out and took her husband's hand in hers.

She spoke first, "Y'all come on inside. We're glad you made it. I've got lunch ready."

Then her husband spoke, "Were y'all able to get some shells for my gun? Hope Ferguson didn't scare you none. Bark's worse than the bite."

And so it was that we entered the world of Frank and Elizabeth Helms. At least those are the names that they used. Rumor had it that they had other names. But it didn't matter. They were just a couple of kids trying to make a life for themselves, living in that old, abandoned trailer, deep in the woods, and deeper still in the spiritual realms of the place on earth they called home. They were a beautiful couple. I've never seen two people so much in love with each other. They seemed to move in perfect synchrony.

Inside the trailer it was dusky dark. It took me awhile to adjust my eyes. Then I was able to look around. The place was immaculate, scrubbed, polished, and orderly. In the middle of the main room was a stove made from a metal oil drum. Off to one side there was a bed made from small, carefully finished logs, about as big around as a man's leg. The mattress was made from fresh cedar boughs and covered by a tight-fitting quilt. The cedar boughs filled the room with their wonderful aroma. Another quilt served as the bed's blanket. I noticed that there was one set of sheets on the bed and another set folded on a shelf, alongside a couple of towels. There were a few cooking utensils, an oil lamp, four stools, a rough-hewn table, a well-oiled saw, an ax, and a shotgun. A few old clothes were hanging on pegs. The collection included a couple of sturdy but well-worn coats. There was also a bookshelf. On it were several books by Hermann Hesse, poetry by Walt Whitman, Carl Sandburg, and Robert Frost, a field guide to wildflowers, a Bible, a copy of David Thoreau's *Walden*, and a world atlas.

Frank was a woodsman. Elizabeth was a wild crafter. He cut wood, hunted, and did a little trapping. She sold herbs and medicinal plants. From time to time they fished. Lunch consisted of a sort of stew that included plants gleaned from the woods and a little bit of fish. Sam and I did not ask what the plants or the fish were. From the texture and flavor of the fish, however, I suspected it was gar. It was a good stew, seasoned wonderfully with some unknown herbs. We drank water that came from a rain barrel. The sod roof was a wonderful filter.

These two young people were living closer to the earth than any I've ever known, and doing so with grace, dignity, and success. It was as if their world was a grand symphony and they were instruments in the orchestra, responding to the moods and directions of an omniscient conductor who challenged them with seasons, the vagrancies of weather, and the moods of the river. The challenges had molded them. Though still so very young, Frank and Elizabeth were masters in their realms.

After lunch we opened our packs and shared gifts we'd brought for them. There were shotgun shells for Frank's old but lovingly cared for single-barrel .410 shotgun, a gallon of oil for the lamp, two packages of cornmeal in sealed plastic bags, dried beans also in sealed bags, two pairs of cotton gloves, some scented soap, and a few items for personal hygiene. The only request had been for the shotgun shells. The rest came as gifts from us and from a few other people who knew that these two kids were trying to live out there in the woods. But we had been careful not to bring too much. Frank and Elizabeth were very proud people and fiercely independent.

Not too far from the trailer was a stretch of forest that had been hit hard by a tornado a few years earlier. An area perhaps a quarter of a mile long and a couple of hundred yards wide had essentially been "clear-cut" by the storm. Most of the trees had been uprooted and tossed like sticks in the wind. When the floods followed, the downed trees had been moved into jumbled piles scattered around the area. With sunlight now able to hit the ground, early-growth vegetation had sprouted. It was a wonderful place to pick blackberries and also fabulous habitat for rabbits.

As Elizabeth cleaned up the table from lunch, Frank, Sam, and I went outside on the porch to get ready for our hunt. Frank slipped on his rubber boots and called for Ferguson. Sam and I rummaged around in our packs for our shotgun shells. I had a Remington 12-gauge automatic inherited from my grandfather. Sam had an equally old Winchester 16-gauge pump. Frank's little single-shot .410 looked like a child's toy next to our cannons. But it was anything but a toy. In Frank's hands it was a lethal, almost sacramental, tool.

His simple shotgun was all he could afford, as were the tiny little shells it fired. And he was very careful with his shooting. If the shot was not a sure thing, he did not shoot. The small shotgun also had another virtue. When Frank shot, even at close range, there simply were not many pellets coming out through the end of his shotgun's barrel. At most, there was only about a half an ounce of shot, compared to well over an ounce of shot from our larger guns. As a result, game killed by Frank was never full of shot or had meat destroyed. His little shotgun was a meat gun, not a sporting arm.

These were the days before deer had been restored to this part of the country. There were a few deer around, but they were so scattered that even seeing one was a special occasion. Although his little shotgun was illegal for hunting deer, Frank always carried a couple of slug loads. He killed deer when he could, but he couldn't count on deer and so did not hunt them. His staples were rabbit, squirrel, and fish. And in addition to hunting, he had several box traps. With them he'd catch rabbits, opossums, and, sometimes, even raccoons.

It would be easy to say that these two kids needed to come out of the woods and join the rest of our rush-away world. They were bright and attractive people. But they'd dropped out of that world. They'd chosen a different way, a quieter way . . . a way that took them into intensely spiritual realms of being. They knew that other world, that "outside world," but only intersected it now at tangents. They didn't seem to be escaping from anything. Rather they were moving toward something.

This was an era, a time in our nation's history when many young people were choosing to live and "farm in the woods" as they plunged ever more deeply into a counterculture. But Frank and Elizabeth were not farming in the woods, and, as far as we knew, they did not use drugs. They didn't need an artificial escape from the world around them. They'd found the world they wanted, a real world, and were living in it. They could have left their world at any time. There were opportunities for them on the outside. But that was not what they wanted. They had paid, and were continuing to pay, a high price for their chosen way, but it was their choice and they were secure in it.

It was all I could do to keep from tempting them with conversation about things going on "outside." Plus, I wondered what would happen to them if they became very ill or had emergencies. Other than walking out of the woods or perhaps taking a raft to go downstream to the river, there was no way for them to communicate with the outside world. And what if they had a child? The questions kept swirling in my mind. Sam would look at me occasionally and I'd look back. I knew that he had the same sort of questions. And yet we knew that we had to keep quiet on these subjects. If Frank and Elizabeth needed change in the future, they'd change. If not, then there'd be no change. They knew what they were doing.

Frank whistled up Ferguson and clomped down the stairs of his porch to the ground where Sam and I waited. "Ya'll ready?" he asked.

Without waiting for a response, he started walking, with Ferguson at his side. We picked up our guns and quickly followed. Frank had a woodsman's gait and was covering ground. He wasn't being rude. He was just focused. We had to stretch to match his pace.

As we walked across the clearing in front of the trailer, through a scope of woods, and toward the area where we'd be hunting rabbits, there was a serious set to Frank's face. This was not a recreational hunt. None of his hunts were recreational. He hunted and trapped and fished because if he didn't, he and his wife didn't eat. He exploited the resources around him year around, paying no attention to seasons or regulations. Everybody in the region who knew about this young couple knew that Frank hunted when he needed to hunt. And nobody cared. The game wardens turned a blind eye and left him alone.

It took us about fifteen minutes to get to the hunting area. It was early afternoon and the sun was bright and warm. We hunted in shirtsleeves. The brambles were thick and full of thorns. We tried to pick our way carefully through them, but in spite of our efforts, we were quickly covered with scratches and dried blood. The trick was to move slowly while Ferguson burrowed through the tangles. After all, finding the rabbits was his job, not ours. Our job was to get into position where we could see the ground and, if Ferguson pushed a rabbit past us, to shoot the thing. So far that autumn there had only been light touches of morning frosts. We needed to keep a lookout for snakes that might be prowling on this warm afternoon.

It took Ferguson about ten minutes to bump his first bunny. We'd been hearing him give an occasional high-pitched bark as he found scent. Then, all of a sudden, there was an explosion of bawling that let us know that the rabbit had been found and rooted out of its hiding place. The chase was on! But it seemed that Ferguson wasn't making much progress. We couldn't see him but were able to keep track of him through his barking as he "put the heat" on that rabbit. Putting on the heat is a relative thing. Brambles aside, Ferguson simply couldn't push very fast with his short legs. It seemed to take forever for him to move any distance at all.

That was actually the treasure of Ferguson. It didn't take long for the rabbit to realize that he didn't need to move fast in front of the dog. It would make its typical rabbit circles, returning again and again to the starting point, but just not be in a hurry about it.

As long as Ferguson kept pushing, the rabbit would keep making the circles . . . until we shot the rabbit.

With the chase now on, we spread out to vantage points where we thought the rabbit might be spotted and perhaps give us a shot. The best stands were atop some of the trunks of blown-down trees. Regardless of where we stationed ourselves, it was important to have a clear area so that we would be able to see the rabbit as it passed through our zone. However, with all the brambles, finding that combination of stand location and clear area was a real challenge. Opportunity would come in a flash and then be gone.

The rabbit made one complete circle without giving us a shot. It had skirted Sam's area but had quickly darted back into thick cover. Ferguson kept on the trail, pushing the rabbit ever forward. It was then that I noticed Frank coming down off of his perch on top of an old tree trunk. He moved directly into the brambles. Once again Ferguson was coming toward us, unseen, but full of music. Frank was directly in line with the chase.

Suddenly I saw Frank's gun come up to his shoulder and it looked like he was pointing his gun almost directly at his feet. Then he fired. It sounded more like a little pop than the typical boom of a shotgun. Frank stayed where he'd stood at the shot. Ferguson kept coming, passed Frank, and then stopped. There was a different sound to his bawling for a moment, and then all was quiet. Frank stepped over to where Ferguson was and picked up the rabbit. It was a big swamp rabbit. It probably weighed five or six pounds.

Quickly, Frank pulled out his pocketknife and made a slit between the rabbit's two hind legs, cutting all the way through skin and muscle and down into the body cavity. Then he squeezed the rib cage hard a couple of times. With his gun unloaded and leaning against a sapling, Frank took the dead rabbit, held it in both hands like a baseball bat, and, with a strong sling of the "rabbit bat," all of the rabbit's internal organs went flying out of the cut between its legs and landed about twenty-five yards away atop a thick mass of bushes. By doing this, the rabbit was field dressed and would start to cool quickly. Frank would not risk the rabbit spoiling.

The hunt continued. The first rabbit had taken us about thirty minutes from the beginning of the chase to the shot. Fifteen minutes later Ferguson had another rabbit going. Sam shot it on the first pass. Frank took the rabbit and repeated the field dressing process. Then Frank said, "That's enough for me, but let's get one more for y'all to take home." Twenty minutes later Frank shot rabbit number three with his little .410 and we started back to the trailer.

All three of the rabbits were swamp rabbits and each would, after skinning and dressing, provide between three and four pounds of meat. Frank and Elizabeth had no way to store meat for very long, and so for them, the rabbits stayed "stored" and fresh out there in the brambles, just as fish stayed "stored" out in the river and its backwaters. It was sort of like the way they handled their "garden"—the forest. In it Elizabeth picked what was needed each day and, except for nuts and acorns, left the rest in the woods.

Unknown to Sam and me, and while we were on our hunt, Elizabeth had been doing just that. By the time we returned from the hunt, she had what she needed for our supper. Frank skinned, washed, and cut up the rabbits and took them to Elizabeth. Then we helped him split wood for the stove. Elizabeth already had a fire going in the stove and was busy with cooking. She was preparing a salad of fresh greens and other wild vegetables and baking a sort of bread from white oak acorn flour. She'd soaked the tannins from the acorns, dried them, and then ground them into flour. She then took one of the rabbits, trimmed the meat from the bones, and prepared a sort of stir-fry dish with the rabbit and some wild herbs. Her cooking filled the trailer with wonderful aromas.

We told Frank that we'd really prefer to leave our rabbit with him and Elizabeth. He resisted at first, then said OK. Then he nodded to Elizabeth and she took the other two rabbits in the pan. As supper cooked, she cut the meat from the bones, as with the first rabbit, but then took the meat and sliced it into very thin strips. She worked the thin strips of meat into a mixture of pepper, salt, and dried herbs. The treated strips were placed into a shallow pan and taken out to the porch, where the sun was still shining and where there was a slight breeze. The pan was covered with thin cheesecloth to keep the flies away. She was making a sort of rabbit jerky.

I asked Frank about the jerky, whether it really was safe to eat it. He said that it could not be eaten like venison jerky. It would dry and stay OK for a few days. But it had to be cooked before being eaten. Having the extra rabbit meant that he would be able to go to the woods with Elizabeth during her wild-crafting ventures for a couple of days. Winter would be upon them before they knew it, and they needed to gather more acorns. They also needed to stock up on pecans and walnuts. In other words, "Thanks!"

After leaving the rabbit strips out on the porch, Elizabeth returned inside to tend to the cooking. Frank brought stools out to the porch for us to sit on. Then he called Ferguson. Sam and I took our seats. Ferguson came to Frank and sat down in front of him. Obviously, this was a routine. Frank got down on his knees, petted the dog and praised him, and then went over him thoroughly, checking for cuts and thorns. He inspected the dog's eyes, ears and gums. Following the inspection, Ferguson got a good brushing and was fed a mixture of boiled greens to which was added a few chunks of boneless fish and a handful of cornmeal. It was obviously a mixture that worked because Ferguson was in perfect condition.

I asked Frank about Ferguson's shots. "Yes," he replied, "Ferguson gets his shots every year on schedule, along with periodic preventative medicine for heartworm and intestinal parasites." Back then I hadn't heard much about heartworms, but Frank knew about them. This dog was precious to him. Ferguson meant the difference between eating and not eating most days. He took care of that dog just like others take care of vehicles, boats, and farm equipment—the stuff they depend on to "make it." Giving his dog a daily exam was like lubricating a tractor and changing the oil in a car.

I asked Frank how many rabbits he estimated he shot in a year. His answer was that he went out with Ferguson four or five days a week and typically their hunts were one-rabbit hunts. Normally, he hunted in the mornings, when it was cool, not afternoons. And, as we had experienced, it didn't take too long to get the rabbits on each hunt because Ferguson knew his business. After the hunts Frank could do other things, like work on his traps and nets, make repairs around the trailer, or help Elizabeth with her wild crafting. And, of course, occasionally he had to go "outside" on business to sell fur or the things Elizabeth collected, and also to buy the few things that they needed. Since he walked, those trips typically were about two days long. He stayed overnight with friends like Sam. Here around the trailer, there was also a lot of quiet time. He read his Bible and books that he borrowed from friends when he went to the outside. Elizabeth also liked to read.

Shadows lengthened. Elizabeth announced that supper was ready. We gathered around the table and took our seats. We bowed our heads. Grace was said.

The meal was wonderful, but it was the quiet conversation that nourished us more. We talked of seasons, the river, and the land that surrounded our lives. We spoke briefly of matters outside. There was a war raging in Vietnam during those times, and it was impossible not to speak of it. We all knew that eventually the war would touch each of us.

There was a long period of silence after we spoke of the war, but it was not uncomfortable. Somehow it helped us regain and reconnect with the blessings of life in the present tense. Frank and Elizabeth clearly understood that the present tense is really all that we have. They had deliberately chosen their way to live in it, a way that fit them.

Sam and I both desperately needed a strong dose of the present tense. Although unspoken, this was the real reason for our visit. We were young men in our twenties, but already our past was becoming fading memory. The future seemed to have a little more certainty because of the war, but still the future was shrouded in some strange, swirling vapor. There were only shadows dancing before us. In those shadows we could sense realms of adventure, fear, and pain, but it was impossible to imagine their true depth, their true power. Now, decades later, having been there, having experienced it, having lived it, I still cannot wrap my imagination around it all. God in His loving grace erases some things and pulls us back into the present tense. Resurrection depends on it.

Following the silences, the conversation around the table drifted in another direction. We talked of storms and floods and dogs and blackberries. We spoke of nets and traps and fish and critters of all sorts. There was no rush in the meal. There was no rush in the conversation. It was perhaps the gentlest meal I'd ever experienced. Everything was soft and full of grace.

After supper, we lingered on the front porch in the dusk and on into twilight. Then, as stars began to blink in the sky now turned black, it was time to go. Sam and I had a pretty long walk to get back to the car. The trail would be dark, but we had lights and knew the way. And, as we said our goodbyes, we looked back at Frank and Elizabeth standing together on the porch. There was no doubt in our minds that they too, absolutely, also "knew the way."

Ferguson followed us to the edge of the clearing, an escort of sorts, to make sure that the people he loved, the people he provided for, were alone again in their world, a world of their choosing ... a world of the present tense. Good dogs live there too.

Passing the Hunter's Torch

...

GROWING UP IN THE SOUTH, I LEARNED AT AN EARLY AGE THAT wealth comes in a variety of forms. Beyond the love of family, our most precious possession is southern culture, a culture steeped in history, literature, arts, mythology, and storytelling—a culture that takes truth and transforms it into meaning. Tightly linked with culture is land. The land does not need to be your own as long as you have access to it . . . or perhaps a deeper connection. Our relationships to the land are, in fact, sacramental. They lead us deeply into the realms of both material and spiritual wealth. Among our sacraments are hunting, fishing, trapping, gardening, working livestock, driving tractors, cutting firewood, killing hogs, picking blackberries, feeding chickens, and swinging out over a creek on a rope.

Our sacraments require particular tools that in and of themselves are treasures because they are the means through which we gain perspective and clarify identity. In this regard, some things are much more valuable than they appear at first glance. Old guns fall into this category, especially if they've seen service in war, and particularly so if they were used in war by family. And, in some circles the most valuable assets in the sacramental realm come in the form of the ragged, drooping ears, long tails, and the rawboned flesh of coon dogs.

People trade vehicles, horses, guns, political favors, and sometimes even farms for a good dog. But cash rarely changes hands. The transactions tend to be within an entirely different economy because few people actually have the cash necessary to purchase a good coon dog. A true champion can be valued at many thousands of dollars. They are the sirens of dreams.

The hunting and fishing magazines I read as a kid really didn't address coon hunting very much. They seemed more focused on upland game, deer, big game, and sport fishing. A boy had to dig very deeply to find things written about coon hunting and coonhounds. After considerable effort, however, I found a couple of trapper/woodsman magazines that had coon-hunting articles and a few novels about people in backwoods rural areas who hunted coons. I treasured these works. I could shut my eyes and envision myself out in the hills at night listening to the music of hounds on a trail, enveloped by deep sky overhead and shadowy valleys and hollows around me.

I didn't have a coon dog and, in my young mind, couldn't imagine ever having enough money to purchase one. I wasn't old enough to drive, and so even if I'd had a coon dog, I wouldn't have been able to go out to the big woods where I'd have the freedom of movement needed for good coon hunting. So I had to connect with the southern heritage of raccoon-oriented enterprise in another way. I built box traps and established a small trap line with them in some woods that extended back behind my house. Additionally, I had a friend who owned a double-spring leg-hold trap, just one. He let me borrow his treasure. I also had an old single-spring trap I'd found on a floating board in a nearby lake that obviously had been lost by some muskrat trapper.

But for all practical purposes, I was a lost soul wandering in the wilderness. There was nobody around to teach me how to trap. I knew nothing about sets, lures, or runs. Although I put in a lot of effort at trapping, I never caught anything in the leg-hold traps, and all I ever caught in my box traps were possums.

Eventually, I returned the double-spring trap back to my friend. He had an uncle who showed him how to set it and within a couple of days, early one morning, I got a telephone call. It was my friend. He had a raccoon in his trap and wanted to know what to do. I instructed him to get his .22 rifle, shoot the coon in the head, and then set the coon out to cool in a secure place. I told him that the coon would be just fine until he got home from school and could devote the time to carefully skinning it.

I don't know why he called me. I'd never trapped or skinned a coon. I'd never even had my hands on one. But he did as I'd instructed and ended up with a beautiful raccoon pelt hanging on the wall over his bed. I was so envious! I so wanted my own coon skin on my bedroom wall.

As luck would have it, there was a woman in the church where my father was pastor whose husband, Mack, was an addicted coon hunter. Mack had several dogs and, apparently, places to go hunting with them. He was a grown man at full stride and really didn't seem to like kids very much. I knew that, but it didn't matter. I wanted to go coon hunting, and as far as I could tell he was the only entryway into the coon-hunting world. So I just kept pestering him day after day, week after week, all one fall season, until . . . finally he agreed to take me, on one condition—I'd carry all the coons we got.

Well, for a boy who wanted coon hunting and who wanted coon skins so bad that he was losing sleep over it, and whose grades in school were suffering as a result of distraction and day dreaming, such an offer was beyond belief. Sure—I'd carry them! Mack just laughed and then told me when and where to meet him.

On the agreed-upon day, my father dropped me off at Mack's house right at dark. We were met at the door by Mack's wife. She escorted us out to the back of the house, where Mack and a hunting buddy were busy loading dogs, lights, and other gear into a rough-looking pickup truck. Mack's coon-hunting buddy was a wiry little Baptist preacher who Mack said was the best tree climber in the county—apparently an essential skill to have on a coon hunt. There was good fellowship and good humor in our gathering. My father was told when to come get me (dawn the following morning) and goodbyes were said.

Then Mack turned to me and said one word, "Ready?"

"Yes, Sir!" I shouted, and headed for the truck.

When I got to the truck I was told that I was to sit in the middle and hold the .22 rifle so that it wouldn't get knocked around. It was a new rifle and Mack didn't want any scratches on it. The dogs were in crates back in the truck's bed. I had sense enough not to talk, to wait until addressed. That seemed to suit the men just fine.

We drove for perhaps thirty minutes along backcountry roads, finally stopping at a big scope of woods. The men began gathering their gear: spotlights, dog leashes, the .22 rifle, and an old cow horn to call in the dogs if necessary. Then they turned out the dogs.

The dogs milled around the truck for a few moments and then were off. It wasn't more than ten minutes until they'd picked up the trail of a coon. They started bawling their heads off. One was deep and resonant. One was high pitched and sort of squealy. The other two had almost bell-like qualities to their calls. It was easy to tell the dogs apart just by their bawls.

The chase lasted less than fifteen minutes. Even though this was my first coon hunt, I could tell by the way the barking changed that the dogs had something very different going on. They were no longer moving and trailing. They had that coon up a tree!

We worked our way quickly through the woods to the tree, and when we got there we entered a world of chaos. The dogs were storming around the tree. Occasionally one would try to climb the tree, "walking" up the trunk and then twisting and falling backward into the maelstrom. They were all clawing and chewing at the tree trunk and making a tremendous racket with their bawling. In no uncertain terms they made it clear that what was up in the tree needed to come down and take its medicine.

Shining the lights up into the branches, we quickly spotted the coon. His eyes reflected the light. Then we shined more light and could see the entire animal.

Mack handed me the rifle and told me to shoot where he had the light pointed. I could see that he was pointing directly at the raccoon's forehead. I put the bead of the open-sighted rifle on that spot and shot. There was a solid "whack" as the bullet struck. Then, to my almost unbelieving eyes, old Mr. Coon came tumbling out of that tree! He was dead before he hit the ground, but the dogs wanted to make sure. They were on that coon in a flash, each dog grabbing a piece of the coon and all of them pulling in different directions. Mack said that it was a "death hold." I was sure that they would rip that coon to pieces.

The preacher rushed to the dogs on one side and Mack rushed to the other side. Little by little, they were able to pry the coon out of the dogs' mouths. Then they handed the coon to me. I was elated! What a coon! This fellow weighed at least twelve pounds— a real trophy. The pelt was prime, thick and glossy. I could already envision it hanging on my bedroom wall. Then we were off again. As agreed on, I carried the coon.

Half an hour later we were back in business again with another treed coon. When we got to the tree, I asked if I could shoot this one also. But Mack said no, that we'd shake this one out for the dogs to kill. He explained to me that unless you let the dogs kill about every other coon, they won't hunt as hard as they should. So I stood back to see what would happen.

The preacher climbed the tree. I'd never seen a grown man climb a tree, but this fellow was a master at it. He was small enough to get way up in the "tippy-top" branches where the coon had gone when he'd seen the preacher start the climb. Then the preacher started swaying the tree, getting more and more sway with each move. I was sure that the top of that tree would snap off, but it didn't. Finally, the coon lost its grip and came tumbling down. As before, the dogs immediately attacked it. But this time the coon was very much alive and fought the dogs with a viciousness I'd never imagined. There was screeching and growling and hollering and shouting. The coon ripped at the dogs savagely and the dogs came back with even more savagery. Ears were torn. Noses were split wide open. Sometimes the fight was just a blur of dogs and coon wrapped together in a screeching, tumbling wad of fur, hide, and popping teeth. But eventually the dogs prevailed and their death hold served its purpose. When it was all over, the dogs were in a trancelike state and wouldn't release their holds. Mack and the preacher had short sticks for such a situation and used them to pry open the locked jaws of the dogs, to get the coon from them.

I'd never seen anything like this. It was primitive. It was gruesome. It made me feel sick. This wasn't what I'd expected. I'd never really considered the violence of mortal combat—beast against beast—or what was at stake when it all boils down to the final common denominator. As a young hunter, I'd always been instructed by my mentors to make clean, quick kills. But that wasn't the objective here in this part of our coon hunt. Rather, the objective had been to stoke the dogs by letting their deepest instincts rule.

I wasn't part of the kill but rather a spectator, as were the men. But I felt responsible for the violence. We'd set the stage. We'd brought the elements together. But in reality we were simply witnesses to a drama, a very basic, fundamental drama that had ancient origins. It wasn't pretty. But it was not wrong. It is what dogs do and have been doing since before they were wolves. It is also what people take dogs into the woods to do and have been doing since those ancient wolves started hanging around camps and following people into the woods in search of prey . . . and since people and wolves discovered synergy in their relationship.

Before there were guns, and even after there were guns but people were just too poor to own them, dogs were essential to bringing home the game. Even when I was a kid, there were people in this economic category who lived in the hills where I roamed. They couldn't afford guns but were fully engaged in hunting with their dogs. They sold the coon hides they collected and cooked the meat for their families. They did the same for possums.

Letting the dogs kill worked, as Mack had said it would. Just as soon as we got the dead coon away from the dogs, they were off as hard and as fast as they could go in search of another. They'd tasted blood and within them—and in me—surged a very strange wind. That wind fanned fires within me, bringing to life tongues of flame and waves of heat that, with the wind, mixed together as echoes from someplace else . . . echoes that reverberated not only in the bawls of the dogs and in the stillness of the winter woods, but also in a place deeper than my soul.

I couldn't deny that something within me that I'd not known before was awakened. I felt it rush through my body and take hold of my mind. I felt like I'd been hunting in this way, with dogs in wild places, for a very long time . . . beyond my years. The echoes enveloped me. I became as one with the dogs, the woods, the night, the kill. I was able to shake off the shock and nausea that had smashed into me during the fight and the kill. I regained my focus. Then I took a deep breath and rejoined the hunt . . . but never to be the same again.

Soon the dogs had another trail full of coon scent and were going in the general direction that led back toward our truck. Almost immediately, we heard them bark "treed." When we found them, they were no more than fifty yards from the truck, dancing around a blackjack oak scarcely more than an overgrown bush, perhaps twenty feet high. Apparently, the dogs had been right on the coon's tail as it rushed across a clearing in the woods. The coon had panicked and had taken refuge in the closest tree it could find. Since this coon was a "shooter," I collected him with the .22—cleanly—with a well-placed shot behind its ear.

We had taken three raccoons on our first stop. It wasn't even 10:00 p.m. The night was still young. I couldn't have asked or expected a hunt any better conducted than what Mack and the preacher had just led me on. I had three fine coons. I liked their heft as I lugged them through the woods and on to the truck. I liked the feel of their thick fur and the stiffness of their fuzzy tails. I liked how they smelled, how their smell blended with that of dogs and men and gun smoke and the night.

There was energy in the night, and the catalyst to release it was the incredible, strangely disturbing, and yet wonderful spirit from hunts and hunters past that swelled within my breast. It felt like I was being passed a torch on some adventure into unknown territory and that it was my turn to carry it for a while.

We loaded the dogs and ourselves back into the truck and took off for new territory. The place where we stopped was a little more hilly than the first, and the trees were not quite as tall. We released the dogs, got our gear, and started out into the woods. Mack then turned and asked me where my coons were. I told him that they were back in the truck.

"Go get them," he said.

It was then that I realized the game. I was to carry the coons, ALL of the coons, the entire hunt. Collectively, we already had more than thirty pounds of coons. I weighed about a hundred pounds. But a deal is a deal. I went back to the truck, got my coons, and returned.

Off we went, with me lugging those coons, out across the hills and hollows, up and down, across creeks, along ridges and through grown-up pastures full of blackberry briars. I didn't say a word. I just bucked down and did my job.

We added two more coons to the bag on that stop. One was a mature boar about fifteen pounds, but the other, thankfully, was a little "kitten" coon about seven pounds. I was a tired boy when we got back to the truck and I dumped our coons into the truck's bed. Both of the men were looking very hard at me. I said nothing at first, but then, after getting my wind back, looked both men in the eye and said, "OK, I'm ready!"

I think that was the ticket. Both men slapped me on the back and then, with grins, reached back behind the truck's seat and pulled out sandwiches and cold drinks, cranked the truck, and off we went to the next place. Apparently, I'd passed some kind of test because they started talking and telling jokes and stories and looking at me and asking me about the sort of stuff I liked to do. I told them I liked fishing and, particularly, setting trotlines for catfish. I told them I ran a trap line with box traps I'd made myself. I told them that I'd gotten to skip school the year before for three days and had shot myself a deer at a big deer camp down in the southern part of the state. I told them once I'd built a raft with Boy Scout friends of mine and we'd floated down a river for fifty miles with our scout leaders, including through a big storm. The two men smiled at each other and nodded.

When we got to the next place, I went to the back of the truck, got a piece of rope, and started tying my coons together so that they'd be easier to carry. The men stopped me.

"No need to do that, son." Mack said. "You've already hauled those five coons enough. We'll start fresh now." And so we did. I had a spring to my step, and it wasn't just because I wasn't carrying those coons.

We roamed those wonderful hills throughout the rest of the night. The moon rose and the stars came out bright and beautiful. We forded creeks and scaled small bluffs. Once, the dogs jumped a deer and ran it until they were out of earshot. Mack called and called with his hunter's horn, and finally the dogs came slinking back to us, tails down and heads low, knowing they'd get some pretty good medicine from Mack, which they did. He cut a switch and switched them all soundly, all the while admonishing them for being the worthless creatures that they were—here he was, the man who fed them, gave them a place to live, kept them healthy, and took them hunting, and this is what he got in return—worthless, deer-running dogs. Then he switched them again.

The dogs understood their sins and came back to him after the switchings with tails wagging slightly, asking forgiveness, which was given. Mack petted the dogs and told them that he really didn't mean all he'd said and then turned them loose again. A few minutes later they struck a fresh trail, and a little after that, we had another coon in a tree. The dogs were pure the rest of the night, netting us another three coons, and never even so much as treed a possum. Mack said that they had just decided to test him when they ran that deer and that they'd expected the physical and the verbal lashing that they got. As a teenaged boy who also ran with a "pack," I could relate very much to such behavior.

We finished our hunt just a little before 4:00 a.m., then called it quits. I was still willing to go on, but Mack said that the dogs had had enough running for one night. Like me, they were willing to keep on going, but also like me, once they were back in the truck, the night's activities started to close in. I tried to stay awake with the men and to listen to their talk. But eventually the talk became more of a drone and then finally the preacher punched me gently in the side, woke me up, and said, "We're home, boy."

There was just the faintest hint of gray in the sky to announce the coming of dawn. The cool winter air was incredibly fresh. The lights were on in Mack's house and as we went inside I could smell bacon in the skillet and coffee in the pot. Mack's wife had gotten up early to welcome the hunters home.

"Did y'all get any coons, Don?" she asked.

"Yes 'um."

"How many?"

"Nine."

Then, with a sideways glance at Mack, she asked, "You carry them all?"

Figuring I wanted another invitation to go coon hunting, I replied, "No, Ma'am, not all the time."

I heard Mack give a sigh of relief. Then, with a smile from his wife, breakfast was served.

Home were the hunters, home from the hills—and the youngest was carrying the torch.

Some Fish Don't Need Wine

...

I WAS STANDING OUT IN THE MIDDLE OF A FIELD IN MY BARE feet, covered with mud and sweat, laying out irrigation pipe, when I met Bert Reynolds. The year was 1973. The only reason I remember the year is because that was the year that I graduated from college and was in the process of plunging headlong into poverty.

In contrast with his movie star namesake, Bert stood about five feet seven and weighed perhaps 130 pounds. He'd served in the US Army during the Cuban missile crisis in the 1960s and was rather matter of fact about that experience. He told me later, after we'd worked together for a while, "Either the world was going to be blown to smithereens or it wasn't. Regardless, as a soldier I wasn't in position to influence the affair one way or another. I just got up every day and did my job. Then one day the crisis ended, and shortly after that I got mustered out of the army."

His slight build was the result of a prolonged, severe childhood sickness, but the sickness had in no way affected his strength of mind and body. He told me what it was, but I've forgotten. I think it was rheumatic fever. But he said that he nearly died and afterwards he just stayed sort of small. Now, at about thirty years of age, and although still a relatively small man, he was as tough as nails in both categories. And yet he was perhaps the most unpretentious man I'd ever met. If you weren't paying attention, you might simply overlook him.

Bert mostly just kept to himself and did his work. But he was not shy or unfriendly. In fact, he was just the opposite. He was full of conversation, but his nature was such that he was absolutely respectful of other people and completely unobtrusive. You had to be around him and work with him to capture the truth of his quickness, endurance, wit.

As the summer evolved, I tried to spend as much time around him as I could. He was an unending fountain of stories and wisdom. When he realized that I was really listening, the fountain grew to be a rushing waterfall. He opened up and I tried to absorb as much as I could.

Bert had a master's degree in horticulture from the University of Arkansas. I was working as a field-hand laborer at the university's agricultural experiment station just beyond campus. My job was to do the lifting, the hauling, the hoeing, the tractor driving, and whatever else I was told to do—including installing and operating irrigation pipe for experimental blueberry patches. That was what I was doing when I first met Bert.

Bert was a blueberry specialist who was conducting research to develop strains that would grow in the South. He pioneered and spearheaded that program even though the eventual credit went to the professors who employed him. Nobody except Bert really believed that blueberries could be grown commercially in the South.

Bert's name and the challenges he overcame are fading in the swirls of agricultural history. Blueberry farms are everywhere across the South now . . . and only a handful of folks remember Bert Reynolds and the role he played in the enterprise. But, frankly, I don't think Bert cares. I don't think he minds obscurity.

In fact, I think that he'd rather it be that way. In all my dealings with Bert, I never saw or heard him take credit for any accomplishments. He was always in the shadows, always in the social "hypolimnion," the deeper strata, away from principal sources of light and energy. He lived at a tangent to the rest of the world. He was out of synchrony with our contemporary rush-away civilization. He really didn't participate very much in the mainstream economy. He didn't need to.

Bert shared his story with me. He told me that he grew up dirt poor. During his childhood his mother taught him wild crafting. It wasn't a matter of passing along quaint cultural knowledge. Rather, it was a matter of survival. With the passage of years, I've forgotten many of the specifics about his family life or even where it was that he lived as a child. But I remember that he knew every edible wild plant, how and where it grew, when to harvest, ways to cook (or not cook), and what the risks (if any) might be. He was the same with wild animals and fish. He harvested and relished what other people tended to think is inferior fare. When he harvested he was deadly serious about it, whether it was plant, fruit, nut, berry, fish, bird, or some other critter.

Bert was unaffected by opinion and attitudes expressed by other people. He'd just shrug his shoulders and walk away. He didn't have much patience for prejudice of any sort—including prejudice regarding food. "Some people are ignorant by choice," he'd say. "That's the worse kind of ignorance."

Folks like Bert, all around the world, are the foundation from which the phoenix rises again and again from the ashes of humankind's civilizations. They are the tenacious ones of our species. They have the common denominators, patterns, priorities, and trends figured out. They are the survivors . . . always have been and always will be. Their wealth is measured not by money or property, but rather by a quiet toughness and a connectedness with the earth around them and with each other. I learned a great deal from Bert during our times together. But it was the fishing that he did that truly impressed me.

Northwest Arkansas is a region replete with fabulous fishing. There are gorgeous streams of all sorts where an angler can go for smallmouth bass. Some of the streams have been dammed. The resulting reservoirs are famous for incredibly good fishing for largemouth bass as well as for smallmouth bass. Below the dams are cold tailwaters stocked with trout. If freshwater fishing amid gorgeous scenery is important to you, the Ozark region is the place to go.

As we worked the fields together, Bert would talk about fishing. But he talked about it in a strange but frank way. I don't think fishing made him happy. I think rather that his fishing, when it went well, gave him satisfaction. When it didn't, he'd shift gears and do something else. But from what I gathered during our conversations, his fishing typically went well. He didn't fish for bass, trout, sunfish, or even catfish. He fished for carp. If he caught something else, that was fine and he'd keep it—I don't believe he ever threw back a fish—but it was carp that commanded his focus.

He had a small home with some land and on that land was a creek. He fished for carp in that creek. He never talked about fishing anyplace else. He fished his creek like he picked vegetables from his garden and fruit from his trees. He fished that creek like he gathered eggs from his chickens. He had his place, creek and all. He lived on it, with it, and from it.

The creek made a tight bend on his property. The force of the current over the years had scoured a deep hole in that bend, which was about fifty yards long and perhaps a hundred feet across. During summer, when the water levels were low, carp congregated in that deep hole. When Bert wanted fish, that's where he went.

I was fascinated by Bert, his lifestyle, and his fishing. I'd caught carp before, but usually when fishing for something else. The ones I'd caught were amazingly strong and fought well. But I had absorbed regional prejudice and considered them "trash fish." If there were folks around who wanted the carp that I caught, I'd give the carp to them. Otherwise I'd throw them back. I knew people who'd throw them up on the bank just to get them out of the water. That was probably appropriate from a fisheries management standpoint, but I couldn't bring myself just to kill them like that, so I threw them back into the water. I never kept one for myself and absolutely never considered eating one. They were "trash."

Carp don't belong in North America. They are exotic fish that were brought to this continent from Europe. In Europe they are considered a fine game fish and good table fare. Early in our nation's history, introducing them to North America seemed to be a good thing to do . . . much along the same reasoning that we now stock rainbow trout and largemouth bass all over the world.

The carp, however, wouldn't cooperate. Fish culturists tried very hard for a long time to get them established and suffered failure after failure. But the culturists persisted until finally the carp achieved a toehold. The rest is history. From that tenuous beginning, carp spread across the continent and became a scourge. They supplanted native species. They rooted and swarmed and muddied waters, making them unfit for other fishes. The flavor of their flesh, considered fine and delicate in Europe, didn't appeal to North Americans, who considered the taste muddy and musty. Nor did North Americans want to contend with the many small bones that laced through carp meat. North Americans want to eat big chunks of bone-free fish—and to do it in a hurry. Europeans, in contrast, enjoy taking their time eating, gently teasing the meat from the bones (or bones from the meat, depending on your perspective) as they sip their wines.

I knew that some people ate carp because I'd been able to give a few of them away. But I'd never been around somebody like Bert who actually focused on them as quality table fare. My interest in the entire affair intensified. Finally, one day, while we were standing ankle deep in mud, attaching together long pieces of irrigation pipe in the university's blueberry patches, Bert said, "Don, why don't you go carp fishing with me on my place this weekend?" I jumped at the chance.

With directions in hand the following Saturday morning, I followed the twisted county road out of town and into the hills. The sun was already up, but the air was still cool. Dew lay heavy on the land. I moved deeper and deeper into the countryside, past hayfields and limestone bluffs. From time to time I'd cross small bridges spanning spring runs and also a few clear water creeks that I knew from experience held good populations of smallmouth bass. It would have been an excellent day to jump into one of those creeks with a light spinning rod and fish for those smallmouth bass. But I continued on.

I thought to myself, "Today I am a carp fisherman." Just that thought stirred something inside of me that felt strange. There was a dimension of prejudice in the thought. The deeper I got into the thoughts about carp fishing, it seemed to me that persons who fished for anything else *but* carp were in some significant way relegated to inferior status. It was akin to saying that if you hunted any waterfowl other than coots, or ate wild game other than raccoon, opossum, or snapping turtle, or did anything else on summer nights but sit around a fire with your buddies listening to your hounds chase red fox, you were disconnected with the real world, from real people, real culture . . . and, frankly, were to be pitied.

Ahead I could see a giant sycamore tree that Bert said would be my landmark. A couple of hundred yards further on there was an old, gray, weatherboard barn. I turned off of the county road at the barn and followed the dusty lane down to Bert's house. What I remember most of all about that place was that it was thick with blackberry brambles.

Bert welcomed me and said that he was ready to go. He was wearing loose-fitting clothing and a slouchy hat, sort of canted to one side. He carried a couple of stiff fishing rods equipped with closed-faced spin-casting reels. He had a few worms he'd dug for bait, but most of the bait he carried was dough balls. There weren't many words. He just started walking.

I followed him along a trail through the blackberry brambles. Eventually, the trail skirted the edge of the creek along a high dirt bank. There were some small, scraggly trees there, mixed in with the brambles. This was where we'd fish. Bert motioned that we needed to walk softly and be quiet. He said that carp were spooky fish, afraid of their own shadows.

I looked at the still pool below the crest of the bank and wondered how in the world the carp could see a shadow of any kind. The water was about the color of milk-laced coffee. It was impossible to know how deep the water was, but Bert said it was perhaps eight feet deep at its deepest point.

Nothing stirred except a turtle that plopped off a log at our approach, and a few blue and green dragonflies darting about on the opposite bank. Indigo buntings called. A turkey vulture circled lazily overhead. The dew had evaporated and it was beginning to warm up. Bert reached for his bait can and stuck one of the dough balls on his hook. There was no other weight of any kind on the line. Nor was there a float or a bobber. It was just line, hook, and bait. He cast the baited hook out into the muddy pool, and as it settled to the bottom, Bert settled down and took a seat in the dirt. The line had a lot of slack in it. There wasn't enough current in the pool to move the bait. If the baited line moved, it would be because there was a fish on the other end.

In a quiet voice Bert said that carp are very sensitive, very smart fish. If they hear a noise or if they detect any pressure on the bait as they work it with their mouths, they won't bite. He also said that if you catch a carp or two, the other carp in the pool will get scared and impossible to catch for a while, perhaps a day or more. But, because carp in the pool tended to be pretty nice sized, it didn't matter. A fish or two was all a person needed for a meal. And that was the object, pure and simple.

I rigged my fishing rod like Bert's and cast another dough ball into the pool. It was getting hotter. Bert didn't move or speak anymore. Bees droned among the blackberry brambles. A skink slipped out of the shadows of the brambles and started across a dusty patch. The dust must have been hotter than that skink had figured it would be because once its feet touched the dust out in the direct sunlight it shifted into high gear and was quickly across and into shade again. I could feel sweat trickling down my back between my shoulders. Cicadas started humming. Wispy clouds hung in the light blue sky, so light blue that it was almost white. Bert's eyes were squinting. I couldn't figure if he was trying to sleep or if he was focusing on something. But I didn't ask.

Then I saw a twitch in the bow of my line, right were it entered the water. There was another twitch, then another. The line began moving, slowly, along the far edge of the pool. I waited until the line was almost tight, then lowered my rod tip. The line started to tighten again and I jerked back—HARD. There was a jerk on the other end of the line that almost pulled me off the dirt bank and into the pool.

Bert quickly reeled in his line. I hung onto my rod as the fish ripped line from my reel. I couldn't see the fish, but from the feel of it knew it was huge. I asked Bert how big he thought it might be. "Oh, a couple of pounds maybe, maybe three, big enough. Don't let it get to that logjam down there."

I was *trying* not to let it get to that logjam, but the fish was sort of in charge of the affair. "You got big enough line?" Bert asked. "About ten pound test," I answered. "Not big enough. Hope it holds." So did I.

The fish showed no signs of tiring as I kept the pressure on it. But it did turn away from the logjam and start back up the creek. I reeled as fast as I could to keep the tension on the fish. It passed us and started going the other direction. That was good because in that direction the bank sloped down closer to the water and, toward the upstream end of the pool, ended in a gravel bar. That would be a good place to bring the fish out of the water. So, with the fish out in the creek on the line, I started making my way along the dirt bank toward the gravel bar.

It seemed the fish was tiring . . . but just a little. When I got to the upper end of the pool, however, I realized that the fish was, indeed, tiring. It still pulled strongly, but it wasn't taking line from the spool of the reel. I kept the pressure on the rod, keeping a good bow on it, letting the rod tire the fish. Then, finally, I was able to work it into shallow water and sort of scoop and kick it up onto the bank. Bert had been right. It weighted almost three pounds.

In the sunlight it glistened like gold. It had patches of scales instead of being completely scaled. Bert said it was an "Israeli" carp, a genetic strain of the common carp, developed the way it was for religious reasons. The scales being the way they were made the fish acceptable for Jews to eat. I had never heard that before but figured Bert knew what he was talking about. More importantly, it was clear to me that the fish was definitely acceptable for *him* to eat.

The fish's body was thick and robust. It was made for power. I'd felt that power, not only in the fish but also in the linkage between Bert, the creek, and the fish—even though I'd caught the thing. Bert was smiling, glad I'd had a good time with the fish and equally glad that we'd have a carp dinner that evening.

When I looked up from the fish toward Bert, I noticed that he already had his gear ready to go. His line was reeled in. The hook was on one of the rod's guides. The bait bucket was beside the rod. We were done.

"That's enough. The carp keep fresher here in the creek than they do in the freezer. This fish you caught will be good."

And so it was. I didn't really pay much attention to how Bert's wife cooked the carp, and I didn't ask. But, served with fresh, sliced tomatoes, summer squash, fresh cornbread, and iced tea, it was delicious. The bones took care of themselves, and, frankly, we didn't need any wine.

I Get There on a Tractor

...

OUT BEHIND MY BACK FENCE, AT THE END OF A SMALL, DEAD-
end alley, shaded by a big water oak tree that I planted many years
ago, an old friend waits patiently for me. We've been friends for
over twenty years and have never failed each other. When we're
together there's a beautiful synergism.

A rusty coffee can covers his exhaust stack to keep rain out of
the engine. The rubber matting on both of the footrests is ragged,
torn, and mostly missing. The hard plastic blades of the radiator
fan show tooth marks from curious mice. The paint is fading and
in some places chipped. There's a dent on one fender . . . origin
unknown. A screw-down drain plug from a boat seals the hole
behind the seat where transmission and hydraulic fluid is added.
The seat cushion is torn in one spot and, along one edge, is coming
loose from the metal binder that attaches it to the seat frame.

My friend is mature and well seasoned. He has guts, good balance, and plenty of muscle. I feed him the right stuff and make
sure he gets his annual physical exam. When he drinks and chews,
I make him rinse his teeth with clean filters. Before and after a
hard day, I rub his joints with soothing grease. Neither of us is
concerned about cosmetics. We're all about function. When he is

healthy we are both happy. I can hear it in his voice when we're cranked up and ready to go.

I am in the tribe of fortunate hunters. I own my own land, a very special fifty-acre jewel tucked back in a quiet corner of Mississippi about six miles from my home in a college town. It is my refuge, my sanctuary. The land and I have co-evolved over the years. I've learned to nudge Nature on it rather than force her—just a suggestion here and there and some "breathing room" for her every so often—and to pay attention to scale. But it took time for me to learn the lessons. And it took a friend: a little twenty-seven-horsepower, four-wheel-drive, diesel tractor.

When we first shook hands we were both fresh from the market and still a little green. I underestimated his power and overestimated what we could do together. He never coughed or sputtered as I piled on the hours, day upon day, with images of a picture-book property groomed to the highest degree.

We mowed, plowed, disked, and planted. Aided occasionally with a chainsaw, we cut trails through the woods and thickets. We worked the slopes of my pond levee to keep the woody vegetation at bay, allowing only grass. I learned that we could mow an acre an hour, more or less, and that keeping twenty-seven acres of pasture looking like a lawn through the entire growing season is virtually impossible and also tremendously expensive.

I had no instructor and so experienced what it is like to have a tractor go vertical when a plow digs too deeply. I know the metallic taste that comes into my mouth as a front wheel suddenly lifts on a steep slope and split-second decisions have to be made to keep from flipping over. My tractor has been an obedient friend, trusting my judgment, even when my judgment was poor. People die on tractors. I understand.

But people also experience the beauty of dreamtime on a tractor. I surely do. I can become lost in its depths. When I climb onboard and fasten my seatbelt, I have never failed to sense something sacramental, a linkage of sorts, founded in faith. I have faith in the machine and my ability to work with it. I have faith that what we do together is not something that is apart *from* Nature but rather something that makes us a part *of* Nature.

Nurturing Nature, and becoming part of it, invokes grace, but it is not cheap grace. Moving into ethereal realms, even on a tractor, demands focus and discipline, in addition to faith. Drift into the dreamtime, certainly, but pay attention to the world around you and to your machine. Listen to the tractor's internal voices as well as your own. Blend them together into a symphony and, when your voices are both stilled, as you pause to refresh yourselves, you will hear Nature also singing. The magic is there.

Birds seem to be the first to respond to a tractor. Egrets appear from nowhere when I'm mowing my pastures. They spiral down from the sky, dipping and slipping to land around me, moving in waves to be the first to capture insects, and sometimes mice, disturbed by the cutting. The egrets have no fear as long as I'm on the tractor. They walk alongside the tractor, seemingly oblivious to my presence—until I stop and get off. Then, suddenly, I become Man and the birds leave . . . lurking somewhere, waiting until the man becomes part of the machine again.

Coyotes, foxes, and deer are not particularly bothered by a tractor. I see them all the time. They let us pass close, watchful, alert, but unafraid. Turtles in my pond don't care either. They keep their perches on logs where they are sunning.

We do not mow pastures until after the Fourth of July. I cherish wild turkey and quail nests, baby rabbits and fawns. We plow, disk, and plant wildlife food plots in late August, hoping for the life-giving rain that can come when tropical storms drift north from the Gulf of Mexico. We clear trails in September so that deer will have clear passageways to the secret places we've created for them. After the first frost, usually in October, we hitch up the "bush hog" and mow meandering strips through protected pockets of tall grass and thickets, creating a mosaic through which a bird dog in fluid motion will bless the golden afternoons of winter.

Rarely do we work more than two or three hours on a given day. There is no need to rush. Rather there is a need to commune, to let the soul of the man ramble through the realms of the never-never land as the machine smoothly rumbles deep in its own soul. In so doing, there have been special encounters.

On one particularly fine August afternoon, when the first hint of autumn drifted through the region, bringing with it the first flights of blue-wing teal and a little welcomed crispness to the mornings, my friend and I were mowing the back section of one of my pastures, preparing it for disking and planting of winter wheat. As we mowed, I glanced up into an old oak on the edge of my pasture, where a hillside transitioned the landscape from open pasture to woodland. Near the top of that tree, on a dead branch, a red-tailed hawk was perched.

The hawk watched us as we worked. The more we mowed, the more restless the bird became. The tall grass melted as the tractor and I worked its perimeter. Then, suddenly, the bird launched—and nailed a cotton rat. I stopped the tractor and watched as the hawk flew back to its perch and ate the rat. When it was finished, I cranked up the tractor again and made another pass through the tall grass. Several cotton rats darted for new cover. Again the hawk attacked and another cotton rat became supper.

We waited again. But the hawk didn't wait. It launched, soared on stiff wings right over me, and called a deep, drawn-out, stirring, two-note call, high, then low. It reverberated in my soul. Immediately the hawk went back to its perch and sat there, watching again . . . waiting again. We made another pass through the tall grass and once again the hawk grabbed a rat. But this time the hawk flew away, with the rat held tightly in its talons. Although late summer, perhaps it had a nest back in the woods someplace. Or maybe it just wanted a midnight snack or something for the next morning's breakfast. It didn't matter really. What mattered were the connections made—man and machine, land and hawk—and an afternoon venture together.

Another evening, as my friend and I put the finishing touches on a wildlife food plot and shadows were deepening, I glanced across the freshly disked ground and saw a snake right out in the open. It was not just any snake but rather a BIG snake, a "tush-hog" snake, perhaps the biggest copperhead I'd ever seen in my life. It seemed to be as thick as my arms and certainly longer than my legs. It was the sort of snake that can kill a bird dog, seriously hurt a child, and mess up a morning's squirrel hunt. The snake was moving slowly but steadily, obviously an old, experienced "patriarch" within the kingdom of snakes.

I'm not really a snake killer. I rarely bother them at all other than to try to catch them and handle them—if I can. In fact, I like snakes, a lot. They are good partners on my property and are part of the rhythms of the place. But this rascal was a dangerous critter, too big, too dangerous to be there.

Normally, I carry a .357-magnum revolver when I'm out working on my property and keep it loaded with a couple of "rat shot" cartridges "up front" for such encounters. But on this day, for some reason, I didn't have the revolver with me. Without the revolver, I had to figure out another way to confront Mr. Snake.

I shut down my tractor and stepped down to the ground. The snake, previously not at all concerned about the tractor, saw me get down. It stopped moving. Then it shifted position and faced me, head raised above the ground, about a fifty feet away.

I looked around for a stick and finally found one. I picked it up, tested it against the ground, and moved toward the snake. The snake held his ground as I approached. I got to within about ten feet from it and saw the snake grow tense. He knew what a stick was all about.

Suddenly, in a fraction of a second, the snake made its move. I had no idea that a snake could move that fast. I've been around lots of snakes, all over the world: cobras of all sorts and sizes, rattlesnakes, Asian and African vipers, cottonmouths, and non-poisonous species by the hundreds, if not thousands. But never in my life had I seen a snake move that fast.

Had he wanted to bite me, there would have been absolutely no way to keep that from happening. But he went the other way, into the forest, into the shadows, and was gone—like an avatar.

It all happened so fast that after the snake was gone I had to remind myself that the encounter had actually happened. I was a humbled man, standing alone on freshly disked earth, stick in hand, taking deep breaths.

As I crawled back up onto my tractor I felt very, *very* small. The universe whirled around me and I came to grips with how vulnerable a man is to forces within it that are beyond control. The snake had been minding its own business. It was I who had forced the encounter. The snake made the ultimate decision . . . not I.

The tractor rumbled and popped and purred in beautiful cadence as I drove it across my pasture to the place where I keep it parked. Once there, I shut down the engine, put a block of wood under the clutch pedal, removed and hid the key, and started walking toward my truck. But before I got to the truck I stopped, turned, walked back to my tractor, crawled back up onto the seat, and just sat there for a while in the dark. Insects were singing. Coyotes called. I heard an owl deep in the woods. Frogs were tuning up for their evening concert.

The snake had not scared me. Rather, it had impressed me. I don't think that the snake was scared either. It had been in charge of the encounter, sort of.

As I sat in that tractor seat, the word "respect" kept coming to mind . . . coming and coming until it flooded me. It wasn't just respect between man and snake. That encounter had simply served as a catalyst. It was something much bigger: respect for earth as place and for earth forces, respect for machine as tool and for machine forces, respect of man as being and for man forces and how they meld, one into another, given the chance.

The tractor was still warm. There was still a little ticking as the engine cooled and metal adjusted itself into repose. I reached over across the steering wheel and patted my tractor. I thought to myself, "He sure is a good friend. And he's taken me to special places on our land, in my soul."

Nobody was looking. I was all alone. I got down, walked to the front of my tractor, wrapped my arms around it, and gave him a kiss—on his forehead, right between his eyes. The coyotes yelped and the owl called again. I think they understood why a gray-bearded man would kiss his friend under the stars of a summer night.

Three Rifles

...

HUNTERS TEND TO REMEMBER A MOMENT OR SITUATION THAT took them from whatever identity they'd held previously into the rich domain of the hunter's world. Most can actually remember their epiphany and, if asked, will tell you the story. Typically, it was experienced during childhood. For a few, however, it may have happened later in life. Whatever the story, we should listen carefully, because it will reveal more about that person than just the circumstances that framed the beginning of an evolutionary journey.

I would like to tell you my story and share with you the magic moment of epiphany. To do so would be somewhat analogous to sharing the moment that I came to know that God is real. But I can't do either one because there were no such moments . . . at least not that I can recall.

Hunting has always been my identity. A fascination for life in myriad forms has enveloped me, comprehensively, from the very beginning. I had no option but to pursue life. To hunt and capture and sometimes to kill, this was how I could come close to life—and also to death—and begin to understand the meaning and the power and the mystery of both. This hunter's pilgrimage has been, first and foremost, a spiritual journey. Only the tools of the hunt have changed over time.

I went from lips to fingers to hands, to spoons and sticks, to tweezers and pocketknives and fish hooks, to sling shots, spears, and gigs, to BB guns and homemade box traps, and on to rifles and shotguns, better traps, fine fly rods, and archery equipment. I have always been consumptive as a hunter, during all developmental stages, because in doing so it seemed that I was brought closer to something I couldn't define but felt deeply. I didn't know the word "sacrament" until later in life. After I discovered matches, at about seven years of age, I'd secretly build small fires in the woods and fields beyond our back fence and cook lizards, tadpoles, little fish, birds, and field mice. I never killed just to kill. I loved life. I celebrated life. Eating what I captured made what I captured and killed become part of me. I sensed it . . . deeply . . . even as a very young child.

There was a connection to something beyond myself that was always there, a source of energy that was so real but that had no name—until I was told as a preschool child that what I was feeling, what I knew, was God. What I'd sensed in me and around me just got a name, and I like names. Now, as an elderly scientist, I still like names and love taxonomy. Names help me love life all the more because I can think about life in some orderly way. Such scientific order is, admittedly, fuzzy around the edges, but still it helps me. And when I learned the word "hunter," back when I was worming my way as a very small boy around our yard and garden on my knees, stalking denizens therein in the weeds and bushes and climbing the branches of fruit trees in our orchard, I knew that was me. There were no epiphanies. I just had a name for what I was.

Hunters, however, can lose their way. They can forget parts of the journey and how these forgotten parts helped them come to grips with their relationships with earth, self, and God. It just becomes so complex over time that the roots of those relationships get lost in the shuffle. The echoes are still there, but we just can't hear them. And yet, somewhere along the way, those echoes were shared with people who cared enough to listen. The memories were never lost, just transferred for safe keeping to special folks whose gifts for remembering tend to burn brighter and longer. Eventually, if the hunter is very lucky, God creates a gathering of good friends, and there is resurrection of the echoes, of the old stories. Thus begins the tale of three rifles.

THE FIRST RIFLE

It was bound to happen eventually, but the way it happened was completely unexpected. It was midsummer. The rolling country-side of north-central Kentucky welcomed me and the rest of my family back to the community we'd called home while my father completed his seminary training. We'd been gone for about a year, down in Arkansas, where my father had accepted a call to serve his first post-seminary church. Although our family's roots were deep in Arkansas, I had no feeling for them at that point. I was eleven years old and my home, the one I missed, was rural Kentucky.

I had been given freedom to roam the wooded hills, the creeks, and fields there. They were days full of discovery. Few rocks were left unturned in the little creek that coursed through a pasture and alongside a small gravel road a hundred yards or so from the parsonage where we lived. It was a slice of heaven for me. Catbirds called softly from the thick vegetation that shaded the creek. Crayfish and salamanders lurked in the still pools. I knew every bullfrog perch and how to approach them unseen. We were too far north for venomous snakes to be of much concern.

As time progressed, I ventured ever further into the country-side. My little creek flowed into a larger creek about half a mile from my house. In that larger creek there were sunfish to catch. The creek was hardly wider than a country road, but to me it was huge, mysterious, and a little scary. It took me nearly two years to work up the courage to actually go wading in it, which, of course, meant I had to swim in it because invariably I'd slip and end up in swimmable water.

I was told that I'd catch polio if I got into that creek. I knew about polio. I had friends in school who were crippled by that terrible disease. But I was undeterred. I saw cows in that creek, and muskrats and turtles, and none of them, as far as I could tell, had polio. I kept my "big creek" ventures to myself and forged ahead as an explorer in love with the wonders of the creek and the woodlands that were along it.

I knew all about explorers, especially Daniel Boone. In history classes at school we were told that he'd started Kentucky when he brought pioneers to the area . . . back before we got our freedom from England and back when Indians were determined to push us back across the mountains from where we'd come. The Indians were also very real to us, although I can't remember ever meeting one during my youth. We could hear their echoes, however, and sensed their ghosts when we prowled the countryside. They'd left their messages everywhere. The plowed fields were treasure troves following rains, full of arrowheads, spear points, hatchet blades, and flint knives. I still have many that I found in those fields as a child.

Many of my friends at school still lived a pioneer lifestyle. They had log homes deep in the woods, in the hollows and hills, with no running water, no electricity, wood stoves, and very long walks to and from where they were picked up and deposited by school buses. There were guns in those homes, and those guns were used to hunt squirrels, rabbits, and raccoons and to protect chickens from marauding varmints like foxes, bobcats, hawks, and owls. There were rifles and shotguns. The shotguns were strictly off limits. The shells were expensive and the guns were too heavy for children. We were very afraid of the "kick" that happened when shooting one of those big guns. But the rifles were different. There were few if any deer left in the region back then, but small game was abundant. The rifles I saw and came to know were all .22 rifles. Boys could shoot a .22 rifle, and we did. It was just part of being a boy in rural Kentucky.

I never asked permission from my parents to shoot a rifle when I was visiting a friend out in the country. It never crossed the minds of my friends or their parents that asking permission would be the thing to do. We just shot and shot and shot. Sometimes we were with an adult, but most of the time we were just by ourselves. I started shooting when I was eight years old and have not stopped. The crack of a .22 rifle is one of the sweetest sounds on earth. And I longed for one of those rifles.

I was a Cub Scout and received the Boy Scout magazines in the mail every month. Every major firearms company in the country had advertisements for their .22 rifles in that magazine. Boys were supposed to own .22 rifles. That was made very clear to us in scouting, when we attended the "men's" oyster stew suppers at church, and in general conversations with the men who whittled away at the benches down by the grocery store where we sold coke bottles (at two cents apiece) that we'd collected along the streets every Saturday morning. But I didn't have a rifle.

After selling my coke bottles, I'd go down to the Western Auto store and look at the rifles until I knew every detail of every one of them. They were just leaning against the wall on a store shelf. There were no locks, cables, or cabinets back then. Guns were tools. Not weapons. But I wouldn't touch them. We were taught as kids not to touch or bother things that didn't belong to us. The storekeeper would watch me and then would come, hand me the rifles, and let me handle them. He understood clearly what was going on. I suppose he figured that, given time, I'd end up getting one for Christmas or for my birthday.

On my tenth birthday there was a beautiful long package on the kitchen table when I got up for breakfast. My heart was pounding. I knew that guns came in long packages. I tore into it and was simultaneously thrilled and disappointed. It was a gun alright, but not a .22 rifle. It was a J. C. Higgins BB gun. I already had a BB gun, but it was a piece of junk that I'd salvaged from a pile of trash. I'd fixed it the best that I could with scraps of wire and baling twine. The new BB gun was beautiful and I loved it, but deep in my heart I knew that eventually I'd have a real rifle . . . someday.

Every week I'd use my coke bottle money to buy a cardboard cylinder containing five hundred BBs. I'd shoot every one of them by the time the next Saturday rolled around. That BB gun became an extension of my body. I knew exactly where it would shoot. I learned all about trajectory and windage and energy. I knew how to shoot it like artillery, using the arc of the shot path to lob a BB great distances. It was deadly on birds and frogs at fifty feet, but I was not a killer. I was a hunter. I rarely ever shot a songbird. In fact, I can only remember shooting two. One was a sparrow that I shot from the steeple of the church where my father was serving as pastor. Our parsonage was next door to the church. The other was a blackbird that I shot at great distance across a pasture. It was probably over forty yards away from me. Both the bird and I were surprised that I'd connected with that shot. The bird was knocked out of the tree and stunned. But when I got to it, I noticed that the BB was just under the skin on the bird's breast. I performed surgery with my pocketknife, gently removing the BB, and then held the bird until it came out of shock. Eventually, I opened my hands and the bird flew away.

What I didn't realize was that I was learning the fundamentals of rifle shooting. It was scaled back to a level that I could grasp, and after tens of thousands of shots from that BB gun, I'd worked out lots of issues in my head and in hand-to-eye coordination. My parents knew exactly what they were doing in giving me that BB gun. Ammunition for a .22 rifle was too expensive for a boy who sold coke bottles for a living. But that boy needed to do a lot of shooting—a whole lot.

My little BB gun did not survive the move from Kentucky to Arkansas. I wanted another, but my parents said just to wait. They encouraged me to spend my time in the woods, on the lakes, and along the creeks that were near our home. I rambled. I roamed. I learned how to paddle boats. I fished constantly. But I didn't have a gun. A hunter without a gun is a miserable creature.

And then we "went home" to visit old friends in Kentucky. One of the families we visited had a daughter a few years older than me named Sue Ellen. She was a notorious tomboy. She rode her own horse and had all sorts of guns. I'd hunted groundhogs with her in the cemetery behind what had been my father's church. We used the tombstones as rests for her .22 rifles, and she had several.

I remember the moment. We were all seated around the dinner table and dessert had just been served. I was trying as hard as I could to be polite and as quiet as possible. The table got quieter and quieter and finally I saw Sue Ellen grin and look around the table at the others gathered there. Something was up. Everybody started looking at me. Then Sue Ellen said, "You want a rifle? I've got one for you."

I was stunned. I was speechless. She got up from the table and soon returned with an old Remington Model 41 Target Master. It was a very much worn but fully functional single-shot .22 rifle. My hands trembled when I took it. My father was proud. My mother was terrified. But she, along with everybody else at the table, clapped. I didn't know what to do. But I knew that I had to get away from that table. I rushed out to the front porch and started crying.

Sue Ellen came out on the porch to be with me. An eleven-year-old boy is not supposed to cry when a fourteen-year-old girl joins him on the porch. But she came to me with my precious rifle in her hands, handed it back to me, and then gave me a hug. "It's yours," she said, "and I'm proud to give it to you. Always remember me when you shoot it." I still have that old rifle and I still shoot it. Every time I do, I remember Sue Ellen. She knew ... she knew what was in my heart and who I was. She'd watched me roam the Kentucky landscape with my BB gun. She'd taught me how to hold steady and breathe and squeeze off shots at groundhogs in the cemetery. She knew.

We left Kentucky later that week and headed back to Arkansas. It was the last time I ever saw Sue Ellen. By the time I got back again to Kentucky, I was almost thirty years old, just back from two years in Southeast Asia as a Peace Corps Volunteer, and a student at the same seminary where my father had attended. Sue

Ellen was grown, married, had children, and was gone when I came looking for her. It was just as well. It is impossible to recapture precious moments. I'll always remember her just as she was, as the fourteen-year-old girl on the porch giving me a rifle and a hug.

Now I had my very first real rifle. It filled my heart and my thoughts. It was an awesome thing to think about. I couldn't shut down those thoughts. They swirled constantly and kept me awake the entire trip to Arkansas. I'd watch the countryside pass, hours would pass, night came . . . and finally we arrived at my grandmother's house on her farm in Mississippi County, Arkansas, about an hour's drive from Memphis. It was very late. In fact it was in the wee hours of the morning when we drove up into her front yard. When we drove up everything was dark. My father knocked. Lights came on, and the door opened to reveal a grandmother full of hugs. I rushed to her, "Grandmother! I've got a rifle!" She smiled and said, "Well, it's about time. Your Uncle Bob will be here right after breakfast to take you out to shoot it."

Grandmother's comment to me about my Uncle Bob coming in the morning to take me shooting did nothing to help me go to sleep that night. I tossed and turned the rest of the night, waiting to hear the first stirrings of my grandmother in the kitchen. When I heard her I quietly dressed and slipped into the kitchen to join her. She had the kitchen door closed so that we wouldn't disturb everybody else. They were all still sleeping.

She poured me a cup of coffee and laced it with thick Carnation evaporated milk. The only time I ever got to drink coffee was when I was with my grandmother. She was a bit of a free spirit, and I loved her for sharing that spirit with me.

"Don," she said, "you've got a wonderful thing with that rifle. You're big enough and I trust you to be careful. Don't bring any tears to this family. That's all I've got to say about this. OK?"

"OK, Grandmother. I'll be the carefullest boy in the whole country. I've just got to hunt."

"I know. You got that from your grandfathers—on both sides of the family. You've got to hunt."

I could hear other's getting up, so I quickly finished my coffee and put the cup in the sink. Grandmother started frying bacon and put some biscuits in the oven. I set the table and folks gathered around. I could hardly eat but managed to choke down a biscuit and a double spoonful of scrambled eggs.

A truck pulled up to the front porch and there was a toot from the truck's horn. Uncle Bob came stomping up the steps, across the porch, and into the living room.

"Hey there! What's this I hear about some new rifle?"

"Yes sir! I've got me one now. Let's go shoot it!"

"That's why I'm here."

So, Uncle Bob, my father, the rifle, and I loaded up into the front seat of the truck and drove to the little store in a community about five miles away named Chelford. Uncle Bob bought a box of .22 shorts. There were fifty shells in the little box. Then we were off adventuring.

There wasn't any talk about guns or hunting or safety or any-thing, except about the crops. We drove and drove, through my uncle's cotton and soybean fields, occasionally getting out to look at the plants. There was nothing to shoot at. I was going crazy but had the presence of mind to stay quiet and bide my time. Finally, we drove across an old wooden bridge that crossed a ditch.

When we got to the other side, Uncle Bob parked the truck and we got out.

My father said, "Get your gun."

I already had.

Uncle Bob handed me the box of .22 shorts and walked with my father and me back to the bridge. There was an old stump sticking out of the water about twenty-five yards away. There was a light spot near the top of the stump.

Uncle Bob said, "Shoot that light spot."

I shot, hit the spot, and pieces of wood and bark spun into the water.

Then, they walked back across the bridge, got into the truck, and drove away, leaving me alone with my rifle, a box of bullets, and a creek full of stuff to shoot at. They just left me, never saying a word. I don't know what I'd expected, but that wasn't it. I was awestruck as I realized that they trusted me, absolutely, with that rifle.

I didn't need a coach or supervision. They knew it. I knew it. And so, finally, I was a hunter, alone in the country with his rifle—my very first rifle. They didn't come back for over an hour. By the time they returned I'd shot all but ten of my bullets. They didn't ask me how much I'd shot. They didn't ask me if I had any left. I had ten priceless bullets in my pocket. I'm pretty sure they suspected as much, but they never said a word. And nothing was said when we pulled back into my grandmother's front yard and went inside for lunch. Not a word. I was the hunter, home from the hunt for the first time, and not a word was said about it. It was the greatest confirmation of identity that any boy, any young hunter, could have ever received . . . not a word said. Incredible. I just walked inside, with the rifle's action open, walked back to my bedroom, put the rifle in its case, zipped it up, closed the bedroom door, and went to the dining-room table for lunch.

A month passed and with its passing came the beginning of school and the beginning of the squirrel season. I wanted to go squirrel hunting very badly, but my mother was adamant that at least for a while I'd be accompanied by my father. That created a bit of a challenge. I was only off from school on weekends, and my father, as a protestant minister, had major responsibilities on weekends. On Saturday he had to visit people at home who had been at work all week. He also had to put the finishing touches on his sermons. On Sunday he had to conduct services at church. There was little if any time to take a boy squirrel hunting. But he did.

It was a frosty Saturday morning and we met the dawn down alongside a little creek called Rachel Creek. When we got there, we encountered two high school boys who were members of our church. They were squirrel hunting with shotguns. It was not a planned encounter. We stayed together for about an hour, and somehow they managed to shoot one old fox squirrel while I watched. I'd never seen a squirrel shot. I'd never seen one tumble to the ground from the top branches of a tree. I'd never had my hands on a squirrel. When they shot that squirrel, however, I felt a switch turn on inside of me. A squirrel hunter was born.

Then we parted. They went one way along the creek and my father and I went the other direction. My father is more of a naturalist and botanist than a hunter. He was poking around in the woods looking at plants when I saw a fox squirrel dart into a leaf nest. I had absolutely no knowledge about squirrel hunting etiquette—that once a squirrel makes it to its nest, its home, you respect that and leave it alone. But I didn't know. All I knew was that there was a squirrel up there in that wad of leaves. So I shot into that nest. The squirrel jumped out, unscathed, ran out onto a branch, and barked. It hesitated just a moment. I'd already reloaded. I took aim, shot, and down plunked Mr. Squirrel, my very first squirrel. When I got to it, it was still alive. I shot it again.

My father, hearing the shots, quickly came over to see what was going on. I stood there before him with my rifle in one hand and the squirrel in the other. He looked at me, grinned, and said that it was time for us to go. I think he'd lingered longer that he'd intended that morning, but was giving me as much time as possible to be in the woods before he went to the church for work.

When we got home, I immediately got a dishpan and my pocketknife and went to the backyard to clean my squirrel. I really had no idea how to do it but was going to do my best.

"Whoa!" my father called. "There is only one *first*. We'll mount that squirrel."

And he did. Fifty years later I still have it, wrapped in tissue in a box full of mothballs in a trunk in my bedroom closet. A more precious trophy never existed.

From that day forward I had permission to hunt alone. I became a shade, a shadow, a rambling, roaming nomad in the woods that started behind our house. I was in the woods, alone with my rifle, until dark settled on central Arkansas . . . afternoons after school, all day Saturdays, and usually also Sunday afternoons. I hunted and I hunted hard. I didn't know how to squirrel hunt and so had very limited success. I couldn't hit a running rabbit with that rifle. But I shot, and I shot a lot at stumps and floating sticks in creeks and, occasionally, at blackbirds. I learned all about that rifle and I learned about hunting. I learned the land and the seasons and the weather and about patience.

For almost three years I hunted this way, day after day, getting better as a hunter and a rifleman. Then, at age fourteen, my father found a farm where I could go squirrel hunting with a friend named Don Flynn. He also had a rifle. And squirrel hunt we did.

We'd take position, side by side in the woods beside a creek, watching the day begin. We'd shoot *at* squirrels as they scampered through the branches. Most were gray squirrels and gray squirrels do not stay put. They are constantly moving. A box of fifty .22 shells rarely yielded more than two or three squirrels in the bag. Our rifles were not scoped and the squirrels were small, generally moving targets. But it really didn't matter. It was the hunting and the shooting that was most important . . . and the bonding as friends.

THE SECOND RIFLE

When I turned sixteen years old I started working after school and on weekends and earning a little money, usually about $15.00 a week. I had to use $2.50 a week to pay for my school lunches. The first thing that I bought was a new .22 rifle and two boxes of bullets. I walked up to the counter of a sporting goods store, put $43.00 on that counter, pointed at the rifle I wanted, and walked out into the streets of downtown Little Rock, Arkansas, gun in hand and two boxes of long rifle hollow-point bullets in my pocket. The gun cost $42.00. The bullets were fifty cents a box. There was no sales tax. There were no firearms sales forms to complete. No identification was required. It was a different world then.

My new rifle was a bolt-action Remington Model 581 that had a five-shot plastic clip. No more rummaging around in pockets for another bullet! Just work the action and you're loaded again. A month later I bought an inexpensive 4X scope and mounted it on the rifle. I paid $8.00 for that scope, a Weaver B-4. It was designed to clamp on the grooves that ran along the top of my rifle's receiver. Some people made fun of me for putting a scope on a .22 rifle. Some said it "wasn't sporting." But I knew better. With that scope I discovered what a .22 rifle can really do. As for sporting,

I wanted to kill squirrels, not wound and lose them. The scope stayed on the rifle. The old single-shot rifle was retired and has remained retired for nearly fifty years. I still shoot it occasionally, but I do not hunt with it.

The first thing that I did was to strip the varnish off of the rifle's wood stock. My friends were aghast that I did that to my new rifle. But, from my experiences in the woods, I'd learned that boys with shiny guns got fewer shots at squirrels than I did with my dull-finished old single shot. I went to the hardware store and bought a can of linseed oil for fifty cents. I still have that can of linseed oil. During the decades I've had it, I've only used about one fourth of its contents, and I am constantly going to my gun cabinet to get it.

Night after night I'd put a couple of drops of that oil on the palm of my hand, sit on the edge of my bed in my bedroom, and rub it all over the rifle's stock. Just a couple of drops is all I'd ever take. I rubbed that rifle stock until my hand was warm, slowly building microscopically thin layers of oil that penetrated down into the wood, sealed the pores in the wood grain, and gave the stock a glow that did not shine. I had to be very careful not to put too much oil on the stock or else it would get gummy and sticky and really never dry. When that happened I had to take a large rubber pencil eraser and remove the gummy residue. Over time that rifle stock became a thing of absolute beauty, and when it got scratched, all I had to do is rub it down just a little with a drop or two of linseed oil to smooth it out again.

Two months after my sixteenth birthday, my rifle was finished, tuned, and sighted in to be right on spot at fifty yards. It was also when Arkansas opened the "Mulberry Season" for squirrel hunting. Spring squirrel hunting was allowed for one month: mid-May to mid-June. I had relatives who owned a large farm about thirty miles away, near the town of Lonoke. It had a lot of woods and was thick with squirrels. I was also old enough to drive and had my driver's license. On Saturday mornings I had permission to borrow the family car and go hunting. I'd finish my paper route by 5:00 a.m. and didn't need to be back to work as an usher at the local theater until 1:30 p.m. I'd pick up my friend Don Flynn about 5:30 a.m. and we'd be in the woods by 6:30 a.m. We'd hunt until noon.

We'd hunted together for several years and had, over time, realized that to be most effective we needed to separate once we got into the woods. They were big woods and the terrain was flat with few features to use as landmarks. But we had compasses and knew how to use them. Shaking hands and wishing each other luck, we'd drift away from each other into the stillness of the spring woods.

There is nothing more lovely or full of life than a spring morning in the South. The birdsong is rich, flooding the world with a symphony of incredible beauty. Cardinals, thrushes, and warblers seem to be in tune with one another, each adding its own score to the movement. The air can be a little chilly and the dew is usually heavy. Good boots are important to keep feet dry during the early part of the hunt and to protect you from snakes later in the morning, when it warms enough to get them active. Although it may be dawn out in the fields and pastures, the woods are still dusky when first entered. This is what you want. You depend on the early morning shadows, and the dew, to help you move quietly, ghostlike, through the woods, with ears as well as eyes probing the branches overhead.

There is no merit gained by rushing. Squirrel hunting is a very slow and deliberate process of melding with the forest and the day. The goal is to become nothing, nothing at all, in that forest. Slap a mosquito and you've just lost thirty minutes of hunting.

Step on a dry stick and not immediately stop and you've lost the edge and probably fifteen to twenty minutes of hunting. Dark and earthy-colored clothing, long-billed hats, facemasks, and gloves are essential. When viewed from overhead, from a squirrel's perspective, nothing down on the ground is light colored . . . nothing. And nothing, other than little birds, moves quickly. A squirrel hunter moving at a pace of more than one hundred yards an hour isn't really hunting, he's just moving.

The new leaves on the trees provide squirrels with a little cover, but they also provide squirrel hunters with waving flags. When squirrels are moving through leafy branches they create micro-storms. But a hunter has to be in tune with the woods to detect them. If it is windy, it is better just to stay home. You won't be able to see or hear those micro-storms, and the squirrels probably aren't moving anyway. A still spring morning, however, is the dreamtime for a squirrel hunter. When the squirrel moves, little showers of dew rain down through the leaves and to the forest floor. The slightest tremor, the faintest scratching of bark, the rustling of leaves, the almost imperceptible vibration of branches, all electrify a squirrel hunter. Predatory instincts, hunting instincts, are activated. There is absolute focus and deliberation to the extreme. The world becomes very, very small—just a patch of woods between predator and prey.

The hunter knows his rifle. I knew mine. When I was in the spring woods, on my Mulberry hunts, I knew exactly what my rifle would do. My trigger finger knew the exact amount of pressure to take the trigger crisply across the sear. My eyes knew exactly the image of the crosshairs in the rifle's scope. My left hand and my right shoulder knew exactly the pressure necessary to steady a rifle when I held it against the trunk of a tree. My mind knew exactly how to regulate breathing, and it seemed also that it could control heartbeats. Heartbeats can be detected when you are holding the crosshairs of a rifle's scope on the eye of a squirrel at thirty-five yards. You squeeze off shots between them.

I remember the first squirrel I took with that new rifle. I'd moved quietly into the woods, perhaps twenty yards, and then stood close to a huge water oak tree, listening, watching, feeling, becoming the hunter. There's a transition that has to happen. It takes a little time to become the hunter. It is a different realm of being than the one lived as you walked across a pasture wet with dew, listening to owls and watching the last of the stars fade. And so I just stood there, rifle in hand, sensing the transition deep within my oversoul.

A small patch of leaves shimmered ever so lightly, high in the canopy of a tree about thirty yards from me. My gaze locked on those leaves. There was a slight purring coming from that patch of leaves. I looked but could not see anything but the leaves, and they'd stopped moving. Had I imagined the movement? I kept looking. The purring came again. I raised my rifle and looked through the scope at the patch of leaves. At first I saw nothing, nothing at all. But then I saw something round. I studied it carefully and realized that it was a squirrel's ear. I looked harder and saw another ear. The squirrel was facing me, head on, quietly purring but not moving at all. I could see its forehead now and its eyes. I centered the crosshairs on that forehead, controlled my breathing, slipped off the rifle's safety, took one more breath, let half of the breath out, and squeezed off the shot.

I heard the bullet when it hit the squirrel and then, suddenly, down came the squirrel in a four-second free fall. There was a soft sound as it hit the ground. I marked the spot, quickly worked the bolt of my rifle to reload, but did not move from my spot beside the big oak. Sometimes another squirrel, previously unseen, will move when one falls like that. I stood there for about a minute, watching, waiting. I could see my dead squirrel on the ground. Nothing else moved. I went to my squirrel. The shot had been perfect. The rifle had been perfect. It was a moment of absolute confirmation.

I took three more fox squirrels that morning, then left the woods to join Don Flynn back at the car. The sun was bright. Cattle moved across the pasture. A slight breeze moved across the land. I could see its ripples, like waves, move the grass on the pasture and the leaves in the tallest trees back in the woods. I was happy with my hunt and with my four squirrels. I could have taken more. The squirrels were abundant in those spring woods, and the morning was perfect. But after four squirrels, I'd unloaded my rifle and left those squirrels for another day, another hunt.

I've never been a squirrel hunter who works for a limit, typically eight to twelve squirrels per day, depending on location and year. In fact, as I reflect across the years, during half a century as a squirrel hunter, I've probably taken a limit of squirrels on fewer than half a dozen hunts. My hunts are more typically graced by three to four squirrels. It is an internal thing of sorts . . . a personal goal that works for me.

But with that rifle, during that same half a century, I've probably shot over a thousand squirrels. I've hunted them all across the South. That rifle has never let me down. It is as accurate as it was the day I bought it. It will keep bullets inside a half an inch at forty yards. I've roamed the Ozark hills with that rifle, plucking gray squirrels from oaks that thrive among the bluffs and down in the drippy hollows. I've taken gray squirrels and fox squirrels of several varieties from the woodlands of Alabama and Mississippi. I've prowled the land of ghosts along the Mississippi River, taking black squirrels from live oak trees that were planted by Confederate president Jefferson Davis. I've taken the orange variety from the rich bottomlands that grace the lower White and Arkansas Rivers. From my farm in east-central Mississippi, I've taken Bachman's fox squirrels, the ones with black heads and white faces, huge squirrels that weighed over two pounds. The earth trembles when they hit the ground.

The crack of that old rifle has announced that the hunter is in the woods on hundreds of still mornings and enchanted afternoons. It has been my treasured companion when the woods were ablaze with fall color, when snowfall put a hush on the landscape, when storms thrashed the trees and me, when soft pastel sunrises pushed the shadows from the spring woods. It has never failed me. It has never jammed when I've quickly worked the bolt to reload. It has never been to a gunsmith for repairs of any kind. It never drifts. It does not like .22 shorts but thrives on .22 long rifle ammo. It shoots half an inch higher at forty yards with 36-grain hollow-point bullets than it does with 40-grain solids. I don't shoot hollow-point bullets. There is no need. My shots at squirrels are head shots. If there is no head shot, I do not shoot. I do not need a new rifle, but I got one.

THE THIRD RIFLE

I am sixty-four years old as I write this. I have recently retired from a career as a university professor at Mississippi State University. I worked in fisheries, primarily river fisheries. During my career I traveled the entire world. I have been privileged to work with thirty graduate students. My first was a student at the National University of Malaysia while I was serving my country there as a US Peace Corps volunteer. I had twenty-nine graduate students at Mississippi State University: seventeen master's students and twelve doctoral students.

Two months after I retired, my students gathered to listen to echoes, reflect, and share the old stories. It was an incredible reunion of an academic family spanning nearly thirty years. My former students are scattered to the four corners of the world, across the continental United States and into Alaska, Asia, Australia, Europe, South America, and the Caribbean. Several are professors at other universities. I'm an academic great-grandfather. And they gathered. For three days they filled my life with joy. We shared meals. We rambled the countryside. We fished. We shot guns. We sat close to an open fire as night settled around us, quietly talking, sharing the tales that through the years have become legend. I told the old stories, stories they've heard before, stories that they safeguarded in their hearts. And they knew my sacraments. In so knowing, on the first evening of our reunion, they, along with family and friends (including Don Flynn, my old hunting buddy), gave me a new squirrel rifle.

They'd come together, knowing who I am, absolutely—that I am a hunter and that my foundation as a hunter is framed with squirrel hunting. They placed in my hands an Olympic-grade Model 1416 Anschutz .22 rifle custom built in Germany. I felt love pouring from that rifle as I held it in my hands. It flooded over me.

This rifle is a precision tool with no equal. It is an extremely expensive rifle. But for me it is more, much more. It is my treasure beyond measure . . . for with it my students, my family, and my friends will be my constant companions, from this moment forward, as I move through forests on my hunts, seeking not only the squirrels but, as a hunter, something more precious: the face of God.

The Grinners of Rachel Creek

...

WHEN A BOY IS OLD ENOUGH TO BE ALONE IN THE WOODS, A world of dreams explodes in his heart and becomes reality. Out yonder, in wild lands laced with creeks, lurk sirens whose never-ending songs lure the boy onto the rocks of adventure. He cannot ignore the songs. They stir every fiber of his being. He must heed them or die a spiritual death.

They are the same songs that swirled around him from the pages of books written by explorers, adventurers, naturalists, and sportsmen, books read by flashlight late at night, gifts from a maternal grandfather who himself knew these ways and recognized a kindred spirit in the boy. They are songs wrapped in images of wilderness, mountain peaks, trapper's cabins, and rivers that flow into the realms of the never-never. And then a miracle happens: the boy is given a shotgun.

◆ ◆ ◆

It was a very old single-shot, bolt-action Stevens .410 that my Great-Uncle Early had kept in his bedroom closet for many years, waiting for the proper time to give it to me. It was the only shotgun he'd ever owned, but with it he had shot ducks, quail, and squirrels. When my father's older brother Bob came of age, Great-Uncle

Early had loaned this gun to him so that he could learn to shoot quail. Eventually, Uncle Bob started using my grandfather Jackson's 12-gauge Remington and the .410 went back to Uncle Early. Now it was mine—a treasure beyond measure.

I was thirteen years old. I'd owned a .22 single-shot rifle for about a year when I got that shotgun. The rifle was wonderful, and with it I went with my father and Uncle Bob to shoot turtles in ditches and even once a squirrel . . . my first. But love that rifle as I did, I knew that as a hunter I needed a shotgun, and now I had one.

There were a few rusty spots on it and some scratches on the stock. I worked hard to remove them, and my father helped. Actually, it was my father who sat up late at night refinishing that old gun for me. He transformed a fairly rough-looking gun into a thing of beauty, at least it was beautiful to me (and still is).

The woods began about two hundred yards behind our house in central Arkansas. I had no idea how big the woods were, but in my youthful mind I imagined that they stretched all the way to Canada and probably beyond. The reality was that they probably encompassed a few hundred acres.

The terrain was composed primarily of rather dry, scrubby oak hills that drifted down to a creek we called Rachel Creek. It had another, official name, but we all called it Rachel Creek. There were bullhead catfish in the pools and little wild bass in the pockets adjoining faster water. The hillsides were rocky and occasionally there would be small bluffs and outcroppings. We called one of the outcroppings Chimney Rock. It was the ultimate goal of many a ramble and hike.

The world was, however, very different along Rachel Creek. It was a mysterious world, dark, lush, and damp. The trees, mostly white oak, water oak, pin oak, and ash, were much larger than elsewhere in the woodland and grew tall and straight. Springs seeped from the hillsides. There were ferns in the shadowy places, thick mats of moss on the rocks, and watercress in the spring runs.

The drier uplands were where we'd find quail and rabbits and shoot at passing flocks of blackbirds. The creek bottom was where we found squirrels and imagined elves, fairies, and leprechauns.

The sirens' songs were loudest to me down by that creek. They pulled me ever deeper into their enchanting realm. Although I now sport a white beard, I am again a boy, every time, when on a ramble along a creek. Give me a creek bottom to explore and then give up on me.

The only thing that drove me out from the bottoms of Rachel Creek as a boy was hunger. Many a day the chill of twilight would find me still a mile deep in the woods. When I'd top the last hill on my way back home, stars would be out. Once home, I'd eat alone. My family would have finished supper long before I'd arrived. But little was said. My parents knew what was happening to me, within me. I was a fortunate boy.

Certainly, I was a hunter, but the sirens' songs that I heard were like a symphony with many movements. One of those movements linked me with the spirit of the first free trappers who probed the wilderness lands of the American West and Canada. I'd read the old trappers' journals and the stories of the fur trade, of lonely lands, canoes, frontier outposts, the diverse Native American cultures and their histories, and the rugged men who put themselves out there on the edge because they needed absolute freedom and relished solitude. I was one of them deep in my soul. I knew that I needed to become a trapper.

I had no money for standard steel traps. I'd found one once down along the edge of a nearby lake. It was summer when I found it, and so I determined it was lost and forgotten. There was no tag or identification on it, so I kept it. But, one trap does not address the needs of a trapper. I needed a trap line with several traps. So I placed the treasured steel trap on a bookshelf in my bedroom and began building wooden box traps.

I had a friend named Joe Peceny who knew how to build them. He was a year older than me, a member of my church, and a fellow Boy Scout in my troop. One Sunday after church I went to his home and he helped me build my first trap. Then he showed me his trap line in a woodlot across the street from his house. As I recall, he had three or four traps out in those woods. I noticed how and where he set his traps and began to think about similar places down along Rachel Creek.

The box traps that we built were of a fairly simple design. Four one-inch-thick boards were needed. Those for the bottom and sides were cut to thirty-inch lengths. The one for the top was cut to twenty-eight inches. The trap was nailed together so that it would be taller than wide. Two smaller boards were then cut from the same stock: one to close the back of the trap and one to serve as the trap's door. A two-inch-diameter hole was drilled on the top of the trap about eight inches from the back of the trap. Then a wooden H-frame made of smaller one-inch by two-inch boards was nailed to the sides of the trap about halfway between the drilled hole on top and the front of the trap. A trigger stick with a notch carved on one side and the trap's door with an eye-screw twisted onto its top edge were hung by strong cord from either end of another one-inch by two-inch board. This board would be positioned across the H-frame. The cord was adjusted on both ends of that board so that when the trigger notch was in place in the hole on the top of the trap, the door of the trap would hang freely and straight above the entrance of the trap. Finally, two cross pieces were nailed across the front of the trap, top and bottom, to guide the trap door as it fell into position and to keep whatever was caught from pushing the door open.

I made four traps. They weighed about twenty-five pounds each. I could carry one at a time in my Boy Scout pack. My trapping area alongside Rachel Creek was just a little more than a mile from my home. It took me two weekends to build the traps and a week to get all of my traps into position. Once all were in position, I baited the traps with apples. I couldn't think of anything else to use.

The sirens' songs were drowned by the song that swelled in my heart as I hoisted my pack with a trap inside, grabbed my little shotgun and a handful of shotgun shells, and set course for Rachel Creek. I didn't have much time because I didn't get home from school until nearly 4:00 p.m. and during late fall and winter the sun would set before 6:00 p.m. It would be dark by 6:30.

I was not quite fourteen years old, weighed about eighty pounds, and stood at a height of just a shade over five feet, one of the smallest boys in my class. But when I was alone with my pack, my traps, and my shotgun, out there in the woods, I was as big as any of the free trappers who had roamed the Rocky Mountain wilderness . . . and in my heart I was one of them.

When I'd get home and after I'd eaten supper and bathed, I'd drift off to bed, certainly tired but still full of energy and excitement. I'd toss and turn, imagining what was happening around and in my traps. I wouldn't be able to check them during mornings because I had a paper route to cover and then there was the business of school.

School, however, was also a victim of my trapping. I couldn't concentrate on my subjects, and during band practice my teacher scolded me for not picking up my oboe after school. I tried to explain. What would have been the use carrying the instrument home? There was no time to practice. I had a trap line to run when I got home from school! My explanation didn't get me very far with the band teacher. I was demoted to last chair in the oboe section. But that didn't amount to much and, in fact, it gave me a sense of peace. I didn't have to worry about anybody challenging me for a better seat.

The only teacher who understood what I was about was my shop teacher, Mr. Larry Hale. He knew that I carried a pocketknife (against the rules) but helped me keep it sharp, saying, "A trapper needs a good sharp knife." I worshiped that man. He helped me understand that some things are more important and of higher order than rules . . . but with privileges come responsibility. I'd heard that before from my father. I didn't betray trust or responsibility, and so I could ramble, roam, hunt, and trap—and carry a pocketknife at school.

My first week as a trapper was tough and disappointing. Something just wasn't right. I couldn't figure it out. I didn't catch anything at all. Every day I'd rush home from school, change clothes, grab my shotgun, put the pack on my back, and head for the woods. Every evening, I'd come home cold and hungry and with nothing to show for my efforts.

Then a cold front moved through the area and with it came rain. Following the front, the Arkansas winter became very cold, with temperatures going down into the single digits at night and rarely getting above freezing during the day. These conditions persisted for nearly a week.

I got fresh apples to re-bait my traps, grabbed my gear, put on my gloves to keep my fingers from getting cold and stiff, and headed out to check the line. As before, nothing was in the traps except old brown and worn out pieces of apple. It was so cold that I kept my gloves on when I cut the fresh apples and pitched them into the back of the trap. I didn't bother picking up the traps and dropping the apples pieces inside. I didn't even bother to touch the traps. Because of the rain, the woods were soggy, wet, and, down by the creek where the sun rarely made it to the ground, the woods were frozen. I had to wear rubber boots to stay dry and warm.

Again I returned home, cold, hungry, and disappointed. I brooded and sulked in the privacy of my bedroom. The next morning, on my paper route, I thought about things and finally said to myself, "To Hell with it!" (junior high school–aged boys spend considerable time practicing vocabulary), and resolved that I'd shut down my trap line that very day after school. My traps could just rot in the woods for all I cared. I was done with it all.

That afternoon I shouldered my pack, grabbed my gun (for what reason I don't know, other than that free trappers carry guns), and headed to the woods. It was a gorgeous afternoon . . . one of those crisp, clear golden afternoons that can quickly change the spirit of a boy, and particularly a boy in love with the outdoors. I kept my pace across the hills and then started down the slopes leading to Rachel Creek and my trap line. I got to my first trap and my heart rushed to my throat! The door was down! Taking advantage of the opportunity to use the results of vocabulary practice, I spoke out loud, "Well, I'll be damned!" It seemed the proper thing to say.

I walked up to that trap and picked it up by the H-frame. There was something very much alive inside. I quickly put it back down and got a stick to poke through the trigger hole on the top of the trap. When I did that there was growling and movement. I got down close and looked through the hole. It was dark, but I could see hair, silver-gray hair. Possum! A real *furbearer*! I poked some more and shook the trap, then turned it upside down and shook it some more. The possum sulled. I opened the trap door, grabbed

Mr. Possum's tail, and dragged him out. He was in full sull, stiff as a board, lips pulled back and exposing tremendous teeth, grinning like the Cheshire cat in *Alice in Wonderland*. I stuffed him into my pack, very much alive but still in his sull. The next trap was also tripped—and the next and the next! All contained possums and all the possums went into the pack—alive. I probably had forty pounds of possums in that pack, but I think I could have carried a hundred pounds!

I put the pack on my back, grabbed my shotgun, and, as twilight drifted down on Rachel Creek, started the climb up to the top of the hill and the long hike back home. From time to time the possums would come un-sulled and I'd have to shake the pack to get them calmed down again. I quickly learned that, when un-sulled, four possums that have been stuffed into a single, rather small Boy Scout pack will start to fight. I was worn out from fighting the fighting possums by the time I got home, in the dark.

As I approached the door to my house, I called loudly for my family to come quickly. Fearing the worst, they rushed out into the carport, where I stood with my pack and shotgun in hand. Seeing me unhurt and obviously happy, they sighed relief and relaxed. I handed the shotgun to my father and then dumped the four possums out onto the carport floor. When they hit the floor they all sulled again, with huge grins on their faces. I can't remember a prouder moment in my life.

I was a trapper now—and *I knew why*! While walking out of the woods, it had dawned on me that when I'd re-baited my traps I was wearing gloves and rubber boots. The rain had washed away all of my old scent and I wasn't putting new scent on, in, or around my traps.

Scent control was the key, even for a possum trapper. Those "grinners" had taught me one of trapping's fundamental lessons.

It was then, as I stuffed my possums back into my pack, stood up, adjusted my load, gave the grinners a shake to calm them down again, and started for the backyard, where I had a cage prepared for my catch, that I realized that the biggest grinner of all was me.

Coming Home

...

THE ELDERLY PILOT OF THE BUSH PLANE TOOK ONE LAST SIP from his can of cola, washed down the crackers he'd been munching on during most of the past couple of hours, banked the Beaver hard to the left, and began a landing approach. Below us were the upper reaches of the Coleen River in the northeastern corner of Alaska. The hills and valleys that framed the river were part of the south slope of the Brooks Range, the northernmost chain of mountains in North America.

Landing a Beaver on a remote gravel bar in Alaska was routine to "Frenchy." He could sense direction and speed of the wind over the gravel bar by the way that the plane responded during the turn. However, rather than making the landing, he simply passed over the bar, dipping his wings from side to side while looking out of the windows.

He'd told me that he'd landed here many times, and so I asked him what he was looking for, why we hadn't gone ahead with the landing. I knew the answer but wanted to hear it from him. His response: "I do not want to drop this plane and two caribou hunters on top of a grizzly bear. I can't replace the plane." There may have been an Alaskan smile hidden somewhere in the wrinkles of Frenchy's weathered face, but if so, I couldn't detect it.

Seeing no bears on or near the bar during the overflight, Frenchy circled back around and brought the plane down onto the gravel. There were a few small bumps as the soft tundra tires hit larger gravel, but, considering the place, it was a remarkably smooth landing, a tribute to experience by a very seasoned pilot. When I'm on one of my Alaskan ventures, given the choice, I want the oldest bush pilot I can get. They will get you where you want to go, if it is possible. And, when you're ready come out, they will come back and get you . . . if it is possible.

As the plane came to a stop, Frenchy spun it around to face the opposite direction. Without much fanfare he got out, opened the doors of the plane, and started unloading our gear. Working together, we had the gear on the gravel, in two piles, in less than five minutes. One pile was mine. The other was for my hunting buddy, Nelson Ball.

Frenchy checked the plane to be sure we had all of our gear then walked over to us and confirmed our pickup date. Then he shook our hands and without another word crawled back into his plane. The plane taxied slowly across the gravel to the far end of the bar, near where we'd touched down during our landing. Nelson and I backed away from the "runway," and when we were at a safe distance, Frenchy began his takeoff. With no extra weight from gear and passengers, the Beaver almost jumped into the air. I doubt that the takeoff took more than fifty yards.

The Beaver roared past us without so much as a wing wobble to wish us good luck. Frenchy was focused. He was headed toward Circle, the small community that he called home, and he wanted to get there before dark. His focus was on supper, a warm fire in his house, and his wife of many years. His gift, a gift from God that he acknowledged, was that "going home" meant seeing the Alaskan landscape sweep beneath his wings. He knew that he was blessed. Although the ingredients that created his ventures came pretty much from the same source every day, the way that they were blended into the mix made each day very special.

Nelson and I watched as the plane headed south, as it became a small dot crossing some tall hills, as it disappeared, as the silence enveloped us. The silence that follows an Alaskan drop-off ushers in an amazing array of feelings, something akin to a perfect blend of spices, a blend of remoteness, aloneness, and isolation . . . a blend that I cherish. I love the sweet feelings that engulf me when I stand beside a pile of gear on a gravel bar or next to some lake, as the autumn sun touches the higher hills with an afternoon brush of gold and the shadows that lurked in secret pockets slip out of their sanctuaries and cast their spells across the valleys. I love the boutique of Alaskan breezes, a mixture of tundra and muskeg, gentle on the senses but with fullness of body. It can only be brought to full flavor, however, when chilled by air seeping down from hills and valleys. I love this flavor, and I especially love how it lingers, how it wraps itself around me when seemingly reluctant twilight vapors, shrouded in misty fogs, gently chase themselves down a braided river channel laced with the remnants of last year's snow.

Standing there in the silence, as day began its transition into evening, I shivered ever so slightly as I savored those flavors washing through my soul. The shivering may have had something to do with temperature, but I wasn't sure. I just was not sure. One thing I was sure of—the shivering was in response from something very pure.

The first order of business was to load our rifles. We may not have seen bears during the landing, but we knew that bears were in the area. There were signs, tracks and scat, scattered all over that gravel bar. The presence of bears is just the reality of being in Alaska. Encounters are to be avoided if at all possible. We were not there to hunt bears. Our mission was to hunt caribou, sort of. For the duration of our venture, the rifles would always have rounds loaded in their magazines but, for safety reasons, never a round chambered until shooting was required. An unloaded rifle is just a stick or perhaps a club. Sticks and clubs do not provide much security in grizzly country. But, frankly, neither do rifles . . . unless you know how to use them and can do so calmly and deliberately if need arises.

With rifles loaded and in hand, we made a reconnaissance hike across the gravel bar to look for a place to camp. It had to be a bear-wise camp. There needed to be a place to hang out, cook, wash, brush teeth, keep food and other smelly stuff, and change into sleeping clothing. There needed to be another area for our tent, where we'd sleep. The two areas needed to be separated by at least fifty yards. We needed filtered water, water that seeped through gravel. We also wanted a good view of the gravel bar, the river, and the mountains that surrounded us—breathing room and visual buffer in the event of a roaming bear.

After about twenty minutes we found what we were looking for. The tent place was on a small, flat spot up on a rise overlooking the bar. There were a few stunted spruce trees scattered about that we could use to help keep the tent stretched tightly and to keep it in place. The wind can blow in Alaska. At the base of the rise was a small pool of clear, clean water. The pool was about eight feet across at its widest point and about thirty feet long. By placing large cobblestones in strategic spots, we could access its deeper places, which were, at most, about ten inches deep, and do so without disturbing any silt. The water in the pool seeped through gravel and had just a little current to keep it fresh. The pool was too small to attract birds or other critters, so potentials for direct contamination were minimal. Past the pool, toward the river, about forty yards away on the bar, lay a big driftwood log. It was big enough for two men to sit on without crowding. On one end were branches perfect for hanging cooking gear and wet socks. Close to the log was a good flat space for a fire. When seated on the log, we could see completely across the bar to the river and beyond and down the bar both ways for nearly half a mile. It would have been impossible to find a more perfect camp for two grizzled, gray-bearded caribou hunters.

Nelson and I were both in our late fifties. We had, through the years, evolved into holistic hunters. We knew the ways of the wild, the wild around us and the wild within us. Attempts to tame us had failed. We commanded the primary tools of our ventures, our rifles, and used them with precision. We knew their limitations and ours. There was great synergism. Rarely did our hunts for big game require more than one shot. Hunting had, for us, long ago become sacramental, revealing purposes, truths, meaning. The taking of game provided a focal point to our ventures afield, but the rhythms of our hunts melded into a broader framework, a realm of being that confirmed our identities as creatures in a created world, engaged in evolutionary processes, components of eternal energy flows. We respected the elements but were not afraid of them. When challenged, we did not give up. We celebrated life and took it to its edge.

I had first gone to Alaska as a young man in my twenties. I roamed the mountains, forests, rivers, and tundra with a pack on my back and a song in my heart. As a young professor in my thirties, I lived in Alaska's interior and taught fisheries at the University of Alaska, moving ever deeper into the rhythms of the region, coming to terms with life in those northern lands, and learning that I belong in those lands . . . more than anyplace else on earth.

I left Alaska for good reasons, spiritual reasons, to accept a position that evolved into a full career as a fisheries professor at Mississippi State University. I left Alaska, but I did not abandon Alaska. And Alaska never abandoned me. Threads of grace connected us through the years. And during my exile I returned to Alaska many times . . . for many reasons. Most of those ventures included hunting trips. I shot caribou on several hunts, and moose and bear and wolf. I hunted deer, ducks, cranes, and grouse in southeastern Alaska. I hunted in western Alaska, throughout the interior, and up beyond the Arctic Circle, past the Brooks Range and on out into the North Slope. And, of course, I fished whenever I could. I traveled by bush plane, dog sled, boat, and foot throughout the state. I understood the transformations that must occur when dropped into wilderness. Time and space take on completely different scales.

North America has a lot of wild places. Alaska has wilderness. There's an incredible difference between *wild* and *wilderness*—and in the mindset that is required to engage those differing realities. Five hundred thousand acres is a huge place in most of North America. It is irrelevant in Alaska.

An Alaskan sojourner must transcend the common realm, the scale that fits elsewhere, and engage entire mountain ranges, entire river drainages, valleys and glaciers that flow into forevermore, tundra and muskeg and taiga without boundaries. If lost, left behind, abandoned, or forgotten, you come out on your own. A hundred miles, a month-long sojourn, is nothing. You just keep on going until you are where you want to be or need to be. You don't quit, ever. Alaska requires gumption . . . and thoughtful deliberation. Never underestimate Alaska or the people who belong there.

Nelson was a kindred spirit. Alaska was also in his heart. And yet, aside from his dreams, he had not yet been there. When we were together hunting and fishing in America's Deep South, we'd talked a lot about Alaska, what it was, what it means. Finally, there was no choice. We had to go there together—and hunt. The privilege of being with Nelson when he finally got to his spiritual home was profound.

Now, on that gravel bar, with the Coleen River rushing from pool to pool and the tundra on the hills shifting from red to purple, as the sun faded and a hawk soared between two rocky bluffs, we were both where we wanted to be . . . where we needed to be. There was great peace in our hearts. The winds whispered our names. The river softly sang our songs.

As twilight settled around us, we settled into our camp, our home for the duration of our hunt. From this camp we'd move out into the world surrounding us. Within this camp we'd weld tightly the links that have, through the generations of humankind, bound hunters together.

First there had to be fire. In my opinion, fire—the ability to create and manage flame—is fundamentally all that separates man from beast. Within a camp, fire purifies physical and spiritual elements. It invokes the dreamtime, drawing us out of ourselves, pulling us ever deeper into the realm of primordial echoes. Truth, honesty in being and purpose, cannot be avoided. And fire encourages its sharing. The fellowship of fire is the foundation of human civilization. The smoke from our fire would be our incense in the cathedral that surrounded us. It would also keep mosquitoes away.

With fire comes food. In Alaska, there is real food and there is "cans." Cans have no place in a hunter's camp. And real food requires cooking, careful cooking with the right kind of fire. When your hunting buddy is a talented chef from Louisiana who specializes in Cajun cooking, one who knows all about fire and brought with him at least five pounds of various spices and herbs in his pack, along with other "essential" cooking supplies, you can rightfully congratulate yourself regarding your ability to properly assess human attributes. But I kept my mouth shut about cans. Nelson was in command of the kitchen. It had to be his call. I shouldn't have worried about cans. Before we'd loaded the plane back in Circle, he'd called for a vote and it was unanimous. There would be no cans on this hunt. Once we had our camp set up on the gravel bar, a second vote was called. It also was unanimous. Nelson was confirmed as cook and I was elected to be the dishwasher and water boy. I proudly reported for duty as Nelson hunkered down over his pack and began to pull out its culinary treasures.

We'd done a little shopping before loading the bush plane and so had a few items to cook, enough for a couple of days anyway. There were also emergency rations, mostly freeze-dried stuff, but they didn't count. Our task was to go forth into the wilderness, as necessary, and secure the basic ingredients for our sacramental meals. The sooner we did that the better. A well-fed camp is a happy camp.

I was conscripted to be first up on the foraging detail. Nelson said he'd work on making camp our home. So, at dawn the next day I grabbed my old rifle and headed into the bush.

My rifle, a Winchester Model 70 chambered for 30-06, is a veteran of many Alaskan hunts, and though weathered, scratched, and worn silvery with use, I trust it and I can shoot it. I know from experience on previous hunts that, with a good rest and 180-grain bullets, I can cleanly kill a caribou out to 350 yards with that rifle. In most other parts of the United States, shots at half that distance are considered long.

There can certainly be close shots in Alaska, but in open tundra, in the mountains, and in the expanses of braided rivers, long shots are oftentimes all you get. The only big game animal I've ever killed at a distance of less than two hundred yards in Alaska was a bull moose that I happened upon in a thicket—at about twenty-five yards. That was too close . . . and also a bit scary.

Reality regarding spatial scale in Alaska dictates that the hunter be able to shoot at great distance, and that, of course, means that the rifle must be up to the task. Mine is. The rifle also needs to have a bit of knockdown power. Mine does. I also drew great comfort on this hunt knowing that Nelson's rifle is better than mine and that he is a better shot than I am. I'd seen him shoot, a lot. However, the extent to which his rifle and his shooting trump mine can only be discussed around an Alaskan campfire.

It was good to be back in the bush, rifle in hand. The day was bright and there was very little wind. The survival pack rode comfortably on my back. There was still ice on the backwater pools, but it would all be gone by midmorning.

The silence was deep and profound. I'd sort of forgotten what Alaskan silence is like. On a still day you can hear the click of caribou ankle bones more than two hundred yards away. You can hear a grayling slurp a mayfly from the surface of a still pool at twenty-five yards. You can hear an eagle scream over the top of a hill a half a mile away. You can hear a rockslide caused by a grizzly's passing sometimes further than that. There's nothing to get in the way of pure hearing.

And the sky—the amazing Alaskan sky. During the night there's nothing between you and the stars, nothing at all . . . and there's so much space between the stars that essentially there's nothing between you and God. And, of course, there's the Aurora, the mystical curtains of shimmering light that in the higher latitudes hang almost directly overhead. During the day the blue overhead can be so deep, especially when you're at higher elevations, that it seems almost to be black. And regardless of elevation, the sky sweeps on and on and on like an ocean with islands of clouds. After spending time under the Alaskan sky, and particularly in wilderness near or beyond the Arctic Circle, it is easy to grasp concepts of infinity and eternity. They make absolute sense.

But mortality is linked first and foremost with the earth. Knowing this, I moved forward, carefully, through the twisted stands of willows, scattered groves of small spruce, and blueberry thickets, slowly working my way to a small stream that ran parallel with the river and alongside a steep bluff. I didn't want to bump accidently into something big that bites (bear) or tromps (moose). It took me nearly an hour to go the four hundred yards from camp to the stream.

I wasn't afraid. I was just aware of my world and of the possibilities of an encounter. I'd had such encounters before, and they are not at all fun. Moving through thick brush and thickets, even with a powerful rifle in hand, is one of my least favorite things to do in Alaska.

My plan was to cross that stream and get on top of the bluff so that I'd have a vantage point. I had binoculars and I intended to find a good spot and spend most of my time scanning the vast, open tundra and distant parts of the gravel bar that faded off into the distance. It is certainly possible to be a successful hunter in Alaska by rambling about the countryside, but, from my experience, the less time spent rambling and the more time spent looking make a lot of difference with respect to success of the hunt.

After making it to the stream, I breathed a little sigh of relief. At least now I could see upstream to my right, downstream to my left, and in front of me—up the bluff. My assumption was that behind me was more or less safe since I'd just come through all that brush. As a scientist, I know that assumptions can be dangerous, but it was all I had, frankly, to believe in. A hunter, a warrior, moves forward and, when possible, takes high ground.

To move forward, to get to that high ground, I had to cross the stream. So I sat down and took off my boots and socks. I did not want wet boots for the duration of the hunt if I could avoid it. The stones were smooth and not at all slippery, but still they hurt the bottom of my feet, and that water was COLD.

The stream was at its narrowest fifty feet wide and the depth was up to my knees. Thankfully, there wasn't much current. I moved slowly, rifle in one hand, boots tied together by their laces in the other hand. The socks were tucked under my shirt to increase the chance that they'd stay dry if I slipped. Wet boots are bad. Wet boots and wet socks are terrible. I had extra socks in my pack, two pairs in fact, secured in sealed plastic freezer bags. There was enough sun that day to keep dry socks on my feet. Wet socks, tied to the outside of my survival pack, would dry in the sun and wind. Dry socks also would wick moisture from wet boots. But a slip had to be avoided. No purpose would be served by rushing. I had to be very, very careful.

By the time I got across the stream, my feet no longer hurt because they'd been numbed by the cold. I sat on the opposite bank and rubbed them for nearly five minutes to restore circulation. They throbbed with pain from the cold, but there were no cuts or bruises. For this I was thankful. I slipped off my sweater, used it to dry my feet, then put my socks and boots back on. The crossing had taken at least fifteen minutes.

Alaska demands deliberation. That crossing would also have been the perfect opportunity for a bear attack. I'd given this lots of thought while I was out there in that stream. But I had not crossed with a chambered round in the rifle. There was more chance of me slipping and having an accidental discharge from that rifle than there was of a bear attack. Had there been an attack, I would have been defenseless.

As I dried my feet and laced on my boots, I thought about probabilities and tradeoffs and life in the present tense—life on an edge. They come with the Alaskan turf. All they do is increase my love for that wonderful part of the world. I am, absolutely, more alive in Alaska than in any other place on earth. I am man there, in dimensions that are but shadows elsewhere. Echoes reverberate across the eons of time. I hear them so clearly when I'm in Alaska, when I am alone there, opening the passageways to the oversoul. The echoes can only be heard through those passageways. And they are as sirens calling me. They call me to keep moving, on into the spiritual land of the never-never. And I do.

I stood up. I straightened. I put on my sweater and the light jacket that covered it. Then came the survival pack. I adjusted it on my back, grabbed my rifle, and started climbing up the bluff to the higher ground. When I reached the top, the wind there whispered, "Well done."

The ground was spongy and had no rhythm to it. The terrain was seemingly cast at random, without any pattern at all. And it was amazingly tight. I'd expected to find more space once I'd made it beyond the bluff. But that was not the case. The entire area was a rag-tag affair that left no doubt that once upon a time a glacier had lived here . . . thousands, perhaps tens of thousands of years ago. Under the tundra I labored across, somewhere beneath me, were the gravel moraines. After perhaps an hour, I realized that this impossible terrain would win if I kept going against its grain. So I turned perpendicular to its flow and within thirty minutes was out of the mess and making some progress to higher ground.

I am no muskeg or tundra walker and particularly not when it covers an old glacial moraine.

Once away from the moraine, I climbed perhaps eight or nine hundred feet to the top of a hill and found a good vantage point to survey the land. Looking back along the route I'd traveled, I could see, but just barely, our camp, perhaps a mile away. I'd worked pretty hard to get that mile. To the southeast was a vast plain. In front of me, and sweeping to the south was the river and its gravel bar, laced here and there with thickets and pools and side channels.

There was a slight breeze from the south. The sun was well up. I was warm and sweating from my trek. I took off my sweater to cool and made myself a comfortable nest up against some rocks, in a place where I could sit and survey the land below me. I had two sandwiches and ate one of them, then drank a little water.

Pulling out my binoculars, I settled into my nest. I glassed the landscapes that lay before me for perhaps twenty minutes and then, enjoying the sunshine and the softness of the thick lichens that cushioned my nest, I dozed off. A little over an hour later I woke up, looked at my watch, and forced myself back into focus. I needed to bring a caribou into camp today. That was why I was out there. Through my binoculars I could see Nelson moving about the camp. He had trust in me that I would keep that focus.

I did not want just any caribou. I certainly did not want to shoot a big bull caribou. I had no desire for another set of huge antlers. I had plenty of those back in my home in Mississippi, from previous hunts. They are beautiful things, to be sure, but on this hunt I was in an entirely different operational framework. I was hunting for the same reasons people have hunted caribou in the Arctic for thousands of years. I wanted meat in camp. Big bulls also are "stinkers." They're so pumped up with sex hormones that they're almost impossible to eat. The meat is tough and stringy, there's too much of it, and it does not taste good. No, what I wanted was a young bull or cow, something that I could easily handle alone and which, with Nelson's culinary magic, would grace our dinners. I'd carry my trophy in my heart, not hang it on some wall. My trophy was, in fact, already where I wanted it. I was part of a day in Alaska . . . the land that I love.

About twenty minutes after waking up, while glassing a valley off to the southwest, I saw four dark forms moving toward the river. There was no question as to what they were and where they were going. They were about a half a mile from where I sat and steadily moving. There was no meandering on their course.

Immediately, I gathered my gear, put on my pack, and grabbed my rifle. I plunged down the hill, back toward the stream, knowing that caribou can move quickly, amazingly fast, even when seemingly just coursing the country. I went straight down. Time was of the essence. I had to set up in front of those caribou if I was to have any chance at all.

In less than five minutes I was at the stream. I looked downstream. There wasn't much vegetation along it. Almost immediately I saw the four caribou cross, about four hundred yards from me. The stream where I stood was shallow and there were big rocks all the way across. I jumped from rock to rock and made it across without slipping or wetting my boots. I was the predator, the nomadic hunter, the primitive man engaged in a fundamental, primordial mission. I was the hunter.

I did not go directly on a path that would transect that of the caribou. Rather I made a broad circle to ensure that I had the wind right and that I had the trajectory of travel right. Some sense deep within me took over. I heard the echoes from my primordial origins. There could be no failure. There WOULD be no failure. I felt it deeply. If ever I'd felt perfect synchrony between man, place, and mission in my life, I felt it then. It was beautiful. There was a sweet spot in my soul that kept whispering, "Yes, yes, yes." And I kept moving . . . flowing across the gravel, through the willows, around the pools, skipping across the small channels, in constant movement, constantly aware of my surroundings, at one with them all. I knew—I absolutely knew that I'd be successful. And I was.

I'd never been where I was. And yet I knew exactly where I was. I could feel it. I could feel the perfect integration of time and space and soul. Although I could not penetrate the mind of the caribou, I knew exactly where they were going. Some primordial voice, flowing through my heart, told me that they were coming to me. And I was ready.

Before me was an off channel from the river. Surrounding that channel were patches of willows. Scattered about were drift logs. I took my stand in the shadows of a thicket. I could hear the "click-click" of caribou ankle bones as the group came closer. I could here hooves on gravel. I could hear the occasional splash as they forded the small channels and pools. They were coming and I was ready. A round was chambered in my rifle.

Love poured out to that lovely rifle, that scarred old friend of many hunts. Say what you will, but I believe that a hunter's tool also has a soul. It doesn't matter if it is a spear, an arrow, or a rifle. There is a soul. My rifle shoots better than I can shoot, especially when it counts. And the encounter with the caribou certainly was an encounter that counted.

Suddenly, they were there. There was a large bull with magnificent antlers, two cows, and a yearling bull. They were beautiful! They burst from the willows and came across a large pool of water, with water splashing and reflecting the glory of Alaskan sunlight. Their heads were held high, proudly. I could see the wild in their eyes and in their wonderful, flowing grace as they came toward me. They crossed the pool and veered to the south, perhaps seventy yards from where I stood in the shadows.

Time stopped when they crossed the pool. My rifle was immediately on the yearling bull. He was exactly what I wanted. He was exactly what our camp needed. The crosshairs of the rifle's scope settled on the young bull's chest. There was just the right pressure on the trigger. The rifle sent its message. The young bull staggered momentarily, then fell at the edge of the pool. I have no idea what happened to the other caribou. I was the hunter. My focus was on that bull. God in Heaven, the whole thing was perfect . . . the place, the rhythms, the angels, the caribou, the rifle, and me. I fell on my knees in prayer. And a hawk screamed—a beautiful wilderness cry.

I field dressed and skinned that bull on the edge of the pool. I spread the skin under the shade of willows and then placed the quarters of meat on the skin. I took one of my socks out of its plastic bag and put half of one of the caribou's back straps into that bag. It would be for supper that night. After washing my hands and my knife in the pool, I shouldered my pack, grabbed my rifle, and headed back to camp. I'd need my big pack to get the caribou back to camp.

The hike to camp along the gravel bar took about an hour. Camp was over two miles from where I'd shot the caribou. As I walked I was full of peace. I had what our camp needed. I had what I needed. I was reconnected, absolutely, to the land and the life that I love. I'd shot one time. I'd hunted one morning. I had one perfect young caribou bull.

When I got to camp, Nelson asked if I'd seen anything. I asked him if he'd heard the shot. He had not. But he knew the ways of the hunter. He knew that I wouldn't have come back to camp without success that day. I handed him the plastic bag with the caribou's back strap and confirmed what he knew, in no uncertain terms. I knew also that he was focused on camp and connecting with Alaska in different ways. So I did not ask him to help me pack the caribou back to camp. He had what he needed to work his magic.

I left my rifle and my survival pack in our tent, strapped on my .44 Magnum revolver, emptied my big pack, slung it on my back, and started back to get my caribou by the pool—alone. Nelson understood. A better hunting partner, a partner so completely in synchrony with the spirit of the hunt, has never existed in this world.

As I approached the pool where I'd cached my caribou, I stopped, checked my revolver to be sure it was fully loaded, and cautiously moved forward, revolver in hand. It had been over three hours since I'd shot the caribou, and with the light but steady breeze that came from the north, that was plenty of time for a grizzly to have picked up the fresh meat scent and come to the bull. A grizzly on a kill can ruin a day, absolutely. If there was a bear, I'd relinquish ownership, no questions asked. That's the way it works in Alaska.

Finally, I got close enough to see the meat on the hide in the shadows fifty or so yards away. I stayed right there, unmoving, for a full fifteen minutes, probing with all my senses for any evidence of a bear. I pulled out my binoculars and looked at the meat. It was all still there, exactly as I'd left it. Had there been a bear, the meat would have been scattered, at least a little, and probably some of it carried away from the main pile I'd placed on the hide.

I breathed a sigh of relief but still moved slowly, cautiously, toward the meat. A raven flew up at my approach. That made me feel a little better. Had there been a bear on the meat, there would be no raven, at least not one that close to the meat. But still I kept the revolver handy, all the way to the meat. Slowly, very, very slowly, I eased the pack off of my back and stood again, listening, looking, smelling, focused absolutely with all my senses on my surroundings. I dared not crouch and lose my field of vision—not right then. I waited another five minutes, standing beside the meat. Then I said to myself, out loud, "Where are you bear?!" And I watched again. I listened again. There was no response. No cracking of branches. No movement of gravel. Pray sincerely and your prayer is usually answered. Mine was. There was no bear. The revolver went back into its holster.

As quickly as I could, I started loading meat from that caribou into my pack. Even though it was a "small" bull, I estimated that I had over a hundred and twenty pounds of meat to deal with. It was a tight fit. But, I wanted to get the entire load back to camp in one trip. To do otherwise would be to invite an encounter with a grizzly the next trip. One trip. Only one trip, if possible. It had to be. Somehow I was able to get all of the meat inside of the pack except one hindquarter. This I lashed to the outside of the pack with rope I'd brought for that purpose.

In Alaska, men do things that they generally do not do elsewhere. Alaska takes us to a higher level, both in terms of expectations and ability, physically and mentally. I cut a stout walking staff from a willow, hoisted that pack full of meat up onto my shoulders, secured the pack's belt around my waist, and hiked back to camp. I was careful. I took my time. I focused on balance. I focused on making it back to camp with dignity and good order—which I did—just as the stars began to blink overhead.

When I entered camp, the fire was going and Nelson had supper almost ready. He was composed but quieter than usual . . .

visibly concerned about my late arrival. He understood the risk
of bears. But he also understood that I'd had to walk slowly and
carefully with that heavy pack. As I surveyed the area around the
fire, I noticed that he had his survival pack, our first aid kit, and
his rifle on our sitting log. His headlight was on his hat. It was
obvious that he was only minutes away from beginning a search.

He quietly said he that was glad to see me, helped me get the
pack off of my back, and, without saying another word, turned
his attention back to the task of preparing our supper. With his
back to me, I detected a little quiet emotion, just a little. He's a
good man. He has a good heart. He would have come . . . into the
dark, alone in grizzly country, looking for me. With his back to
me, he stirred a pot of beans and put a lid on it. Then, setting the
caribou back strap to simmer slowly at the edge of the fire on some
coals, he got up from the fire, turned to the sitting log, picked up
his survival pack, the first aid kit, and his rifle, and walked back
through the dark, up the little rise, to our tent.

Nothing was said. Nothing needed to be said. Nelson wasn't
gone long, just a few minutes . . . just long enough to do what
almost all men do when their hunting partner returns safely from
the Alaska bush with a load of fresh meat on his back in the dusky
dark. They have to have few private moments. I understand, absolutely. I've been there. I've had to have those quiet, private moments
alone in the dark. Bears are real, very, very real. In fact, as I was in
the final stages of writing this chapter, I received a message from
my brother, Scott, that a friend of his had just been killed by a
grizzly while skinning a moose.

I did not hunt after killing the caribou. There were other deep
currents to address. I fished for grayling in the river, shot ptar-
migan, and, in general, puttered around camp and the gravel bar.

Nelson and I made forays together along the river. We watched the sun rise and set. We marveled at the stars and the silence and the sky. We nurtured our fires, in camp, in our hearts.

One morning, during breakfast, near the end of our venture, while we were sitting on our driftwood log by our fire, I notice a couple of caribou wandering south of camp.

"Nelson, can you kill a caribou with your rifle at three hundred yards?"

"Yes."

"Get your rifle and look down yonder."

The shot reverberated among the hills and echoed from the bluffs across the river. That morning Nelson came home too.

The Vicarious Holy Grail

...

HAVING LOGGED OVER SIXTY YEARS AS AN ANGLER AND MORE than forty years as a professional in the sciences, addressing management of aquatic resources (particularly fisheries), there is a tendency in some circles to think that I might know what I'm talking about in these arenas and be able to do things in fisheries—to make things happen. As an angler, I've caught lots of fish. As a scientist, I've conducted lots of fisheries research. I've written papers, given presentations, directed master's theses and doctoral dissertations, and even served as president of the American Fisheries Society, the oldest and largest professional, scientific society addressing fisheries in North America. I've worked throughout the world, on every continent except Antarctica. I've provided management recommendations based on science and salted with experience. I can speak with authority and conviction. Regardless, I've been humbled in the pursuit of my personal Holy Grail: catching a two-pound bluegill from my Mississippi farm pond.

When I was an infant, my father held bluegill under my nose so that I'd imprint on them. When I was a young child, he would take me with him as he traveled throughout the southeastern United States as an aquatic weed–control specialist. During one such venture we went to the Auburn University experiment station in

Alabama. It was there that I met Dr. Homer Swingle, the father—some would say "deity"—of farm pond fisheries management.

I can only remember meeting a kindly old man and spending a long day looking at lots of ponds while my father and the old man talked about stuff. Thirty years later I completed a PhD in fisheries at Auburn University. Only then did my father tell me who it was that we met that day on the pond bank.

I was hired by Mississippi State University because of that Auburn University training. During my career in academia, the work I did drifted into lots of other sorts of fisheries, but the foundation of it all was Dr. Swingle's work with ponds. There were certainly variations on the theme, but the core elements stood the test of time—carrying capacity, species interactions, functional groups, growth, body condition, recruitment processes, harvest strategies—and they served me well as frameworks of professional operation.

The fishing pond that I have out on my farm is just a tad larger than one acre. I stocked it with bluegill and largemouth bass using recommended rates and schedules. The pond is well protected from poaching. I work hard to ensure that water quality is good. I provide high-quality supplemental feed during the growing season. I create habitat for spawning and recruitment. I carefully manage harvest, maintaining "bass-crowded" conditions and releasing bluegill over nine inches long until body condition of the larger bluegill begins to decline. Then, very carefully and slowly, I remove a few of the big scrappers—with a wonderful, custom-built, 2-weight fly rod—until body condition in these larger bluegill improves.

This small pond fishery is a fairly simple system: just two fish species: one predator (largemouth bass) and one prey (bluegill). I have control over access and environment (or so I think). I know the scientific and popular literature addressing farm pond management and fishing. I consult with colleagues. I invest time, money, and materials. I administer prescriptions in accordance with both the science and the art of farm pond management. And . . . while I can consistently grow and catch thirteen-inch-long, thirty-ounce bluegill, I have not been able to break thirty-two ounces!

Now, just for reference, a thirteen-inch-long bluegill will cover a standard piece of typing paper (eight and a half by eleven inches) top to bottom, side to side, quite nicely, thank you. Pull a sheet out of your desk and take a look at it. A bluegill of that size will double my lightweight fly rod and bring joy to my heart. It will make me late for church, work, and family events. When I've caught and released a dozen or so of these fabulous fish in an hour or less on light tackle, my mind soars into ethereal dimensions.

But, the reality is that I have failed . . . so far. I have not been able to achieve my goal, my Holy Grail: catching a two-pound bluegill. And it isn't about fish genetics either. Bluegills over two pounds in weight, fish having essentially the same genetic characteristics, are swimming around happily in various aquaria. I go to these places, stare at these fish (I swear they stare back and seem to grin.), and then, humbled, I walk meekly back to my pickup truck that's been baking for a few hours out in the summertime sun.

Frankly, however, there's probably something good, perhaps purposeful and destined, especially if you are a Presbyterian (which I am), about failing at so simple a task, and particularly so after putting all of my so-called expertise to work, expertise garnered over an entire lifetime of angling and an entire career in the field of fisheries research and management. Once again nature wins! Once again, as a scientist and as an angler, as mortal man, I've been humbled by natural variation, by elements in creation that are obviously and clearly beyond my control.

And yet, being a man of faith and hope, a man salted with more than just a little stubbornness, I have not been able to let the dream of a two-pound bluegill fade . . . to just let it go. I knew that there had to be a way either to make peace with the dream or to discover the secret to its attainment. I kept asking myself the questions, "What is the missing element, or elements, if any? Is it even possible for the dream to be realized?"

Then, after a few months of suffering, months of sleepless nights, I experienced an epiphany. I realized that I was up against nature and that for acceptance and healing to occur I needed to share the dream, and the lessons garnered in pursuit of it, with a young mind ripe for philosophical pollution.

It was then that a miracle happened. My sister Sally called me and asked me if I'd take her grandson, Julian Franks, fishing. It was divine intervention and I knew it. So I seized the opportunity, and a few days later I took Julian to my pond, placed a long, light-weight pole in his hands, put a worm on his hook, and told him to "have at it!"

He patiently listened as I explained the value of patience and persistence and dedication to a dream. He endured my recounting of the history of the pond and of how ponds work. But his focus was on the cork in the water and the twitches that indicated something astir out there in the murky depths.

Oblivious to the present tense, I continued to ramble on and on, sharing insights and accumulated wisdom (?), inundating Julian with pontification from his white-bearded great-uncle and retired professor, an old man steeped (for better or worse) in the arts of pond fishing . . . and seeking (privately) to find some sort of peace within the his soul about the entire situation. Julian said not a word. He was fishing.

Julian lives *way up north* in Memphis, Tennessee. He doesn't get many chances to go out into the wilds on adventures. This venture to my pond was the second time in his life that he'd gone fishing.

Julian's third fish that afternoon on my pond was a thirteen-inch-long, two-pound bluegill! It was a beautiful fish, robust and healthy. I just stood there, stunned and speechless on the pond bank, and stared at the fish of my dreams. My dear sister Sally immediately took her grandson's fish away from us, put it on ice, took it home with her, and announced that she would have it mounted for him—so that we will all remember the day forever.

A sister's love for her brother takes on rare form in the Deep South.

Sanctuary

...

THE OLD BRICK CHURCH STOOD SILENTLY UNDER THE MAPLES. There was absolute stillness under a sky that reached forever to and beyond the stars. The moon was still up, casting deep shadows.

I stood alone on the front porch of the parsonage, cup of coffee in hand, looking over at the church in the shadows. I could hear geese overhead. Stepping down from the porch, I walked across the lawn to the church's front door, dug into my pocket for my keys, opened the door, and stepped inside. As my eyes adjusted to the darkness, I could see the communion table. In the center of the table was the brass cross I'd placed there following yesterday's worship service. Moonbeams somehow penetrated the stained glass windows and reflected from the cross. I shivered slightly. I knew that I was not alone. And . . . I kneeled in prayer.

There would be no classes today. Seminary students were free on Monday. It had been a demanding week. Beyond my classes and the endless reading and writing assignments, I had responsibilities as the pastor of this little church in northern Kentucky. Tuesday through Friday I drove south to Lexington Theological Seminary, one and a half hours away. Classes began at 8:00 a.m. Typically, it was dark as I pulled out of the parsonage's driveway every morning and dark when I pulled back into it every evening.

My little flock understood the demands. But still, I was their pastor. And I loved them. When called, I was there. And the previous week had been a marathon. It seemed that my congregation had been plagued by issues and misfortune.

There had been a serious car accident that had injured one of my parishioners. He would be hospitalized for a long time. Somehow, someway, someone had to harvest his tobacco crop. I'd organized a team and we'd been able to put the crop into his barn on Saturday. I was exhausted after the harvest, as I sat at my kitchen table with a bowl of soup and a grilled cheese sandwich, putting the finishing touches on my sermon.

Right after the worship services another parishioner's tenant house had caught on fire. As a member of our community's volunteer fire department, I rushed to the scene. I got there first. The house was ablaze. The man who lived in the house was screaming that his little girl was inside. The only possible way to enter was through a back window. I'd broken through the window and entered.

Once inside, I shouted to the man, asking where his daughter was. He answered that she was on top of his dresser. His girl was not in the house. He was wanting her picture! I grabbed the framed photograph and jumped back outside through the window—just as the flames engulfed the room. They licked at my hands and singed the hair on my arms as I dragged the man away and to safety. Then I stood him up and slammed my right fist into his face, just as the fire truck arrived! Nobody said a word about the preacher punching out that man—they did not dare. Nor was a word said when the man and I sat together under a tree later that afternoon and polished off the last of the communion grape juice together. It was the only thing I had with me in my old car to drink.

Every night there'd been counseling sessions, mostly dealing with marital issues and alcohol. Rarely was I in bed before midnight. The seminary didn't flinch. And neither could I. The courses forged ahead. After the counseling sessions, I turned to my books and my typewriter. And each morning I met the stars as I drove the lonely back roads to theological enlightenment. They'd become friends.

I breathed deeply and arose from my knees. It would be a good day . . . a day of resurrection. I was going squirrel hunting.

One of my church's members had a large farm with several hundred acres of hardwood hills. The streams that coursed the property melded ultimately with the Ohio River. I had permission to hunt and ramble out there. I didn't need to call. I could just go whenever I wanted, or needed, to reconnect.

The property was about a fifteen-minute drive from the parsonage. That was enough time for me to drink a cup of coffee, munch a sausage biscuit, and make a spiritual transition. I think that Jesus probably would have carried a .22 rifle on his wilderness forays had such rifles been available. I think he also would have enjoyed fly-fishing. I know absolutely that he would have enjoyed rambling across those hardwood hills. And, sometimes, as I moved through the forests, rifle in hand, I sensed that he was right there with me as I engaged the rhythms of the earth and squeezed off my shots.

One of my seminary professors, a dear friend named Rosco Pearson, agreed with me. He'd made it absolutely clear, in class and elsewhere, that it is not necessary to be pious to love and serve the Lord. To put it mildly, our hallway and classroom discussions about rifles and loads and particularly good shots were frequently at variance with orientations framing the spiritual lives of some of the others at the seminary. He particularly liked shooting groundhogs at great distances with his .222 rifle. We didn't mean to be offensive. We were just being honest. Rosco was the only man I ever knew who could smoke a pipe, chew tobacco, and drink coffee simultaneously. And, strangely, he was the only professor I had in seminary who started and ended his lectures with a prayer.

There was just a bit of gray light announcing the coming of dawn when I parked the old Rambler station wagon at the edge of the pasture and shut off the engine. We'd had a light frost the previous week, but most of the leaves were still on the trees. In the morning's stillness I'd be able to hear and see the leaves shake and tremble as squirrels moved about. The leaves would also allow shadows to linger in the woods for a little while. As a squirrel hunter, I knew that I could use those shadows to my advantage.

I loaded three clips for my rifle, eighteen bullets in all, put two of the clips into my jean's pockets, and snapped one into the rifle. Working the rifle's bolt, I loaded the chamber, then clicked the safety to be sure that it was on safe. Then, with the words of the poet Robert Frost echoing in my mind—"The woods were lovely, dark and deep . . . and I had promises to keep"—I drifted into the forest and began moving slowly down alongside a drippy hollow. I too had "promises to keep."

After about fifty yards I paused beneath a big oak, senses probing the forest that surrounded me. I could hear the swishing of branches and, looking directly overhead, saw a fox squirrel. He was a big fellow. He'd move out to the end of the branches, cut an acorn, then move back to more stable places to eat. He was straight over me. It was an impossible angle for shooting. I'd either have to move away from the tree, away from the squirrel, to get a better angle and a steady rest for the shot or wait until the squirrel moved to another tree.

It was unlikely that the squirrel would move to another tree, not for a while anyway. He had what he wanted right where he was. The morning was too precious to me to stay put and wait. So I decided that since the squirrel wasn't going to move, I'd have to do the moving . . . carefully, quietly. The squirrel had all the advantages.

There was another large oak twenty yards away, to the east. If I could get to that oak, I would have the dawn light to my back and the tree's trunk to use as a steady rest for my rifle. The challenge was to get to that tree undetected. It was a tough assignment. But I'd been dealing with tough assignments the entire past week. The man, the hunter, focused and moved toward that tree.

I timed my moves to coincide with the squirrel's movements. When the squirrel moved out to the ends of the branches, he was preoccupied with food and balance. His old tail twisted and jerked as he moved further out. He wasn't looking down. He was just trying not to fall.

The leaves on the ground were damp, so I could walk without crunching them. There still were shadows among the trees. There was a small maple tree about halfway to the oak. When I got to it, I clung to it, trying to meld with it, to become part of that tree. The squirrel continued his business in the oak behind me, back and forth along the branches, pausing occasionally on the larger parts of the branches to survey his world, then taking off again for another acorn.

I drifted from the maple and slowly eased toward the other oak. Finally, I made it and just stopped. I wanted my breathing to resume. I also wanted the beating of my heart to quieten. It had seemed obscenely loud the past ten minutes. To shoot the rifle well, I had to be in control of both my breathing and my heart.

Carefully I took position with the oak's trunk to the right. I held the rifle steady against that trunk and waited. The squirrel was not moving. I also did not move. Then there was a flicker of movement near the first oak's trunk, about halfway up the tree.

The fox squirrel was suspicious. Something (me) had caught its attention. I waited, rifle ready. Through my rifle's scope I could see the squirrel's tail, but that was all. The squirrel was hiding on the other side of the tree. I clicked the safety of my rifle on and off several times, trying to mimic the sound of a squirrel cutting a hickory nut or acorn. That did it. The fox squirrel couldn't stand the thought, the possibility, that another squirrel had invaded its territory. It sidled around to my side of the tree and plastered itself, head down, against the tree's trunk.

I quickly put the crosshairs of the rifle's scope on the squirrel's head, controlled my breathing, and squeezed off the shot. The crack of the rifle was swallowed by the morning. It was followed by a thump as the big fox squirrel hit the ground. It kicked a couple of times and then was still. Confirmation, resurrection of the hunter. I was a participant in the eternal drama of energy flows. I took a deep breath, still in position . . . watching, alert. There might be another squirrel in the same tree—and there was.

The squirrel I'd just shot was not the squirrel I'd first seen. As I watched, that first squirrel resumed its forays out into the branches for acorns. The one I'd shot, the one now dead on the ground at the base of the tree, had been an intruder into the first squirrel's domain. The rifle's crack and the thump of the intruder squirrel on the ground had not in any way alerted that first squirrel to a potential threat.

Quickly I worked the rifle's bolt again, ejecting the spent cartridge and reloading a fresh one. The squirrel was out on the end of a branch, cutting an acorn. It was within a clump of leaves. I could see the leaves trembling, but I could not see the squirrel. My focus was locked on that clump of leaves. And I knew the squirrel's pattern. It would come almost to the tree trunk, then stop by a knot on the branch and eat its acorn. I waited, motionless, ready.

Seconds later the squirrel emerged from the leaves and began moving back along the branch. It stopped at the knot and turned, facing me. My rifle's crosshairs were already on its head. The rifle spoke again. The squirrel tumbled through a four-second free fall and hit the ground hard. There was no movement. A perfect shot.

I walked over to the tree and tucked two big, beautiful, Kentucky fox squirrels into the game pocket of my shooting vest. The sun rose. Blue jays began calling. A downy woodpecker hammered away on a nearby dead branch. I whispered a quiet prayer of thanksgiving for the morning and the place and the opportunity to be out there in the hills as a part of all that surrounded me.

My self-imposed limit during those days as a seminary student was three squirrels per Monday morning hunt, considerably fewer than the legal limit. But three fox squirrels are more than enough for a single man, especially if that single man has a couple of hundred pages to read and an essay to write by the end of the day. My plan was to use the squirrels as the basic ingredient for a deep-dish casserole that would last me all the coming week. I had one more squirrel to go.

The hollow I followed was a maze of rock laced with ferns and moss and framed in wonderful old trees. It was steep terrain and really not conducive to stalking. There were squirrels there in the hollow, but to hunt them would require taking a stand and waiting for the woods to forget my intrusion. I didn't want to do that. I wanted to move. I needed to move. I wanted to stalk, not wait. And so I continued, ever deeper into the mystery and magic of the woods on that fine autumn morning, searching for terrain that would allow me to hunt squirrels as a stalker, not an ambusher.

At the bottom of the hollow the woods flattened, just a little. Down where the hollow fanned out there was a small grove of hickories that I knew squirrels were working. It was good stalking country. When I reached that grove, I slowed to my hunter's pace, quietly moving from tree to tree, looking, listening, feeling the pulsations of life that surrounded me. The shadows were now gone, around me, within me. I was nearly there . . . in all of its dimensions.

It didn't take long to locate another squirrel. It was in the tippy-top branches of one of the hickories. I checked my rifle to be sure that it was loaded and double-checked the rifle's safety. Moving like a panther, quietly across the ground, using small trees and the occasional downed treetops as cover, I closed the distance between the squirrel and me. It was a perfect stalk. I took position, held my rifle steady against the tree where I was standing, and waited.

The squirrel moved from one high branch to another, then, in fluid motion, came down that branch and stopped, with a hickory nut in its mouth. I controlled my breathing, slipped off the rifle's safety, put the crosshairs of the rifle's scope on the squirrel's head, slipped on the safety, and lowered the rifle.

I had my three squirrels. Two I carried in my hunting vest. One I carried in my heart. I stepped away from the tree, turned around, and began walking back through the sanctuary of the autumn woods, blessed by the sacraments of hunting, restored by communion with the predawn stillness, and resurrected at sunrise in the sacred space, the holy ground of those Kentucky hardwood hills.

First Light

...

THE HUSH ON THE LANDSCAPE WAS LIKE A BLANKET COVERING the earth. There was absolute stillness on the pond. The breath from an emerging dawn had yet to stir its surface. Shadows were deep. They called to me as some mysterious dark sirens in the sea of a January morning. In the hush, their call was deafening and yet so clear: "Come, come closer—come to us." And I did. I was powerless to do otherwise. I am a duck hunter.

With my dog Hank, a wirehaired pointing griffon, I sloshed through shallow water along the edge of my pond, out to my hiding place at the edge of a small island. Once we got to the island, there was a slight rustling of grass and leaves as Hank settled into his place. The rustling only intensified the spell, the silence, the hush that wrapped itself around us.

I took off my hunting coat and hung it and my shotgun on a cut-off branch of a sapling. Earlier in the season I'd made the peg from the branch for that purpose. Then I reached under a cedar tree for my small bag of decoys. Pulling the sack behind me, I waded out into the pond to set the spread. I needed to get the decoys as far out into the middle of the pond as possible so that they'd be seen by ducks that might pass overhead. If they were too close to the island, they wouldn't be as obvious, particularly at first light.

This meant that I had to wade out until the water was nearly to the top of my waders. I could feel the water pressing against me, ever tighter as I went deeper. I could also feel the mud on the bottom of the pond sucking at my boots. I could not rush. I had to pull my feet slowly from the grip of the mud as I moved. I knew that within a few steps of where I was working the pond would suddenly become much deeper. I had to be careful. I took my time. I moved cautiously and deliberately. There was no reason to rush and risk a slip, a fall, an end. But the water wasn't that cold. If I slipped, if I went under, I could probably escape from my waders. Probably . . .

There were only six decoys in the sack, but for my pond that's enough. Once the decoys were set, I stepped back a few yards to look over the spread. When I did this I noticed that the distance between each decoy was almost exactly the same and that they were much too clumped. That's pretty common when I'm setting out decoys on a very dark morning. Without thinking, I get into a rhythm, a stepping pattern, as I feel my way across the pond's bottom. I put out a decoy, take a couple of careful steps, perhaps three, put out another and so on. As I do it I think I'm scattering them, but I'm not. So, after looking over my spread, I had to go back to it, jumble up the decoys in a more random way and also spread them little more.

When I got back to the island, I pitched the empty decoy sack under the cedar, gave Hank a head scruffle and a pat, retrieved my shotgun and hunting coat from the sapling peg, and climbed across a log to my shooting place. I looked over to Hank and he looked up to meet my gaze. He also seemed to sense the magic of the hour, the place, and the mission at hand.

The quiet reestablished its reign. Tucked among thick brush at the edge of the small island, with the cedar as our backdrop, Hank and I probed the darkness in front of us. Although the decoys were set in open water, maybe only about twenty yards from where I stood, I could only imagine them. They were as lost in the shadows as my thoughts. I looked again at Hank. He was carved in stone. He was born for this moment, just like me.

There was a faint whisper overhead as stiff wings moved the chilled air. Unseen, but known to us, the source of the whisper sent its messages rushing into our hearts. As we listened, a tiny droplet fell from a twig into the water at my feet, the soft yet clear sound of its impact amazing me as I strained my ears in an attempt to keep on hearing the vanishing whisper of wings. Tiny wavelets from the droplet's union with the greater universe of the pond moved only inches before becoming lost in the expanse of the pond's surface. As an ageing university professor, a man on the threshold of retirement, I understood.

Before me was a twisted willow about ten inches in diameter. Its main trunk had broken away years before during an ice storm, leaving only the horizontal branch in front of me and a ragged, vertical hole where the main trunk once had been. Over the years, the hole got deeper as the wood rotted, ultimately becoming the perfect place for me to put my coffee mug. I reached now for the mug that was nestled in the hole, grasped it firmly by its handle, lifted my camouflaged facemask, and slowly took a sip of coffee. The coffee was still warm, almost hot. It felt good going down.

Drinking fine coffee on a winter morning is a wonderful vice. I took another sip, smacked my lips, wiped my beard, and replaced the cup in the willow branch hole. As I did so, a sleepy Carolina wren bounced to a small twig practically in front of my face. It perched there for a few moments, as if to say "good morning," and then flitted away.

On most mornings the wren comes to greet me just a few minutes before the pre-dawn woodcock flights across my pond. When the woodcock fly I know that shooting time is near and that ducks will soon be on their way. The wren also lets me know that all is in good order, that I'm hidden well enough for a duck hunt . . . and also still enough.

Looking back out across my pond, I wondered to myself why it is that *all year long* there is morning wind to ripple the surface of my pond—except in December and January during my duck hunts. I need morning wind and the ripples to give "life" to my decoys. Otherwise, they are just fake plastic ducks sitting out in the water more as something to scare ducks than to attract them. But it seemed to me that during the duck season my pond's water is almost always as thick and smooth as quicksilver and refractory to all but the most direct and sustained winds from the east. Lifeless decoys sometimes work OK at first light, but certainly not later on.

Then I chuckled quietly, reminding myself that the pond is as it is for deliberate reasons. It is purposefully protected from all but east winds because, in addition to being a duck hunter, I am an avid fly fisherman with a strong focus on bluegills in this pond. I've never fished well with an east wind, so my pond is situated accordingly. It is tucked back into a corner of my farm, surrounded on three sides, to the north, west, and south, by dense, mature woods so that the wind will be blocked for my fishing. The reality is that *all year long* the wind does *not* come strongly across my pond during early morning hours, unless, of course, there's an east wind or a pretty decent blow.

A dark form passed overhead. Adrenaline rushed momentarily through me. Then I recognized the bird as a woodcock. The woodcock was a sort of muezzin, calling me to morning prayer. But it was too late this morning for that purpose. I was already in a state of prayer . . . with the morning's stillness as my sacrament.

I returned to my thoughts about fishing. All I could think about was that fly-fishing for bluegills in my pond would be excellent. The winter had so far been warm and the fish were still pretty active. Normally, my bluegills would be "iced down" by this time of the year, making them harder to catch. But this year they were still feeding and growing well in the relatively warm water. In fact, I could even see some bluegills rising at that very moment, sucking up small midges that were emerging close to the island where I stood—and from the size of the swirls, they seemed to be large fish. The stillness this morning would be perfect for casting a fly rod. If I were fishing, I think I'd use a size 12, beaded nymph, tied with fox squirrel hair and . . .

Another whisper of wings resurrected the duck hunter, and thoughts of fishing vanished as smoke in a windstorm. Instinctively, I gripped my shotgun and glanced up. I could see the ducks, just visible overhead and seemingly showing some interest in the pond, perhaps even the decoys.

The sky had faded from black to a dark shade of gray during my mental sojourn into the realms of angling. I'd been so intent on mental images of an arched two-weight fly rod that I'd barely noticed. Now, with my focus regained, I strained my eyes and my ears to maintain sensory contact with the ducks. Was it all imaginary? I strained harder. The whisper of wings faded, then was lost, and then returned, louder now, ever more constant, ever more distinct . . . clearly, they were coming. I kept my face down and looked over toward Hank. Still a dog of stone, only his eyes moved, following the ducks with senses I could only imagine. I carefully checked my watch—five minutes more until shooting time.

The ducks circled over the pond one more time, made a wide swing out over my pasture, and were gone. I knew where: my neighbor's pond out in the open expanse of his pasture, beyond my north fence line. Ducks feel safe there. From that pond they can see a very long way.

These had been big ducks, probably gadwalls. But gadwalls are suspicious and generally hard to get to land on my brushy little pond. So I really wasn't disappointed. Early passovers by big ducks are fairly typical on my hunts. To use the old Cajun term, big ducks shot on my pond are *lagniappe*, a little something special. On my pond, duck hunting is almost exclusively wood duck hunting. And that suits me just fine.

Suddenly, in a rush and flurry of wings, three wood ducks hit the water hard, right in front of me, not twenty feet away. Hank held his ground, trembling. Two more were making their final, twisting turn and were coming right in, working the shadows wonderfully to their purposes. I could only get glimpses of them as they came ripping in past some thick brush on another of my pond's islands, but that was enough. Even though it was still very dark from a practical, human perspective, it was now legal shooting time, and so, from a duck hunter's perspective, time to click into action mode.

One of the ducks coming in was darker than the other. I knew that this darker duck would be the drake of the pair. I shot instinctively, not deliberately, and the duck folded and hit the water with a smack. I lost track of the other flying duck, but at my shot the three wood ducks that had landed on the pond in front of me flushed. I couldn't see them at first because they flew low, down in the shadow of my pond's levee. But then they came up into the "light" (a relative term) and I was able to get a shot. Down came duck number two—something of a miracle, frankly. The surviving ducks grouped, ripped through the treetops beyond my pond, and then, of all things, circled around and came right back over me. I shot a third time as they passed but missed.

I looked over at Hank. He could see the second duck I'd shot out in the pond about thirty yards from us, flopping in the water. He wanted to go get that duck and was trembling and tense but knew he had to wait. He'd look at the duck and then glance up at me. I only played the game a few seconds before I gave him the release command. He was holding well, but I could tell that he was about to come unglued. So I said, "Back!" Immediately, sixty pounds of fuzzy-faced dog hit the water and started churning across the pond. As I watched, the flopping duck regained its composure, got its compass bearings, sat upright, and actually started swimming a little. Apparently, all I'd done was break a wing.

Hank was about halfway to the duck when the duck saw the dog. The duck stretched it neck and I could almost sense it saying to itself, "Oh my gosh!" Then it made a beeline for my pond's levee, which was only about five or six yards from where it was swimming, and, to my almost disbelief, scrambled up the side of the levee, scurried across the top, and was gone!

Hank kept on swimming, got to the levee, picked up the scent of the duck, and also vanished. I just stood there. There was nothing I could do to help. I could only imagine the drama that was unfolding down in the bushes on the other side of the levee. Three or four minutes later, Hank popped up from behind the levee with the duck in his mouth. The duck was still very much alive. I could tell because it was holding its head high as Hank carried it.

Hank paused on top of the levee, looked at me, looked at the pond, and obviously said to himself, "I don't think I'm going to swim back across that pond with this live duck. I'm walking around the edge of this pond to where our hidey hole is on the island and coming across from the back side, where the shallow water is."

I've never admonished my dog for using his brains so gave no commands. He trotted around the pond, sloshed through the shallow water over to our island, and gave me the duck. I praised him, petted him, and then said, "Hank, old buddy, you're not done. Back!" He looked up at me and I could tell he was thinking, "By golly, you're right, Boss. We've got unattended business." Out he went into the pond again, grabbed the first duck I'd shot, and swam back to me with it. I put both ducks beside the willow tree where I was standing. Hank returned to his sentry post. I glanced at my watch. We were about fifteen minutes into shooting time.

A kingfisher swept across the pond, chattering and rattling. The early morning shadows were almost gone. Fog crept across the pasture and swirled on the water. In the distance I could hear geese. The entire world was wet, drippy, and incredibly still.

Again my thoughts drifted . . . this time to deer hunting. I'd only taken two deer so far this season and needed another to top off my venison supply for the year. But the rascals had gone almost completely nocturnal. I just wasn't seeing them when I went to my tree stands for late afternoon hunts. Of course, I reminded myself, I might see more deer if I'd quit sleeping in the stands. The two I'd shot were taken immediately after waking up from a nap and discovering them standing out on the edge of one of my farm's small clearings. I wondered if perhaps my snoring had attracted them. I don't think I grunt when I snore, but I'm not sure.

I reached for my coffee mug. The coffee was cold. I poured what was left of it out and looked around. The two wood ducks I'd shot, both drakes, were so beautiful. I do love them so much, and also the pond and the woods and the fog and the quiet and the shadows and the first thin light drifting over the world . . . but most of all I love the hush that comes to a man's soul on a winter morning when he is in synchrony with the rhythms of the earth. Blessings do flow on a duck hunt.

A flock of blackbirds flew overhead. Their flight signaled that wood ducks were all down now. From many years of hunting, I've learned this. So I took off my facemask, unloaded my gun, and put the two wood ducks on my duck stringer. Then I turned to Hank said, "OK, Hank, the ducks are done. We're done. Time to pick up and go back to the other world."

I slung my shotgun across my shoulders, hung the ducks around my neck, and crawled across the log to get my decoy sack. After climbing over the log, and after a prayer of thanksgiving for divine assistance in that regard, I hung my coat, gun, and ducks on the tree-branch peg and waded out to get the decoys.

As I was picking up the decoys, smug in my "expert" knowledge that the morning flight was over, two wood ducks landed right among the last three decoys I hadn't yet picked up, right there in the open water beside me, not ten feet away. I just stood there, as still as I could. The ducks looked at me. I looked at them. Then I said, "Hi there. Y'all sort of messed up, didn't ya?" They looked at me, then at each other, and—rather rudely and without responding in a civil way—got up in a flurry of wings and flew away. The hen said some things as they left that I will not repeat.

After the ducks flushed, I tried to explain the evolutionary significance of the event to Hank, but he wasn't impressed. He was busy rooting out field mice in tall grass beside the pond. I understood the distractions of youth and, with a smile, sighed. Then I shook my head and resigned myself to the reality that some treasures can only reside in an older hunter's heart. It would seem that even Hank, my best hunting buddy, didn't care that I can snore up bucks and, with him as my witness, am now also confirmed as a pretty decent wood duck decoy. Nor, in his youth, does it seem to matter to him that it has taken over half a century of hunting for me to reach this level of perfection.

I looked up to the trees surrounding the pond. The topmost branches were brushed with gold. First light. And all the magic was there.